GRAMMAR AND COMMUNICATION
FOR CHILDREN

A **CORRESPONDENCE COURSE** is
available for this book.
Call 1-877-75LEARN ext 2720 to order!

Based on the Works of
L. RON HUBBARD

To the Parent or Teacher

Important information about the usage of this book is written on pages 469–471. Familiarity with and application of the data in that section can help your son or daughter or your students get more out of the book.

Published by
Effective Education Publishing
11755 Riverview Dr.
St. Louis MO 63138

www.AppliedScholastics.org
Toll-free: 877-75LEARN

ISBN 1-58460-009-8

Printed in the United States of America

Important

How to Study This Book

Before you start to study this book there is something very important that you should know about studying. This will help you get the most out of this book.

The thing to know and to always keep in mind as you are studying this book is to *never go past a word you do not fully understand.*

When someone goes by a word he doesn't understand then what he is reading can become confusing. He can think that he is not able to learn what he is trying to learn. And also, this is the *only* reason why a person gives up on studying something and quits.

The confusion and trouble with understanding comes *after* a word that was not understood.

Have you ever come to the end of a page and realized you didn't know what you had just read? Well, somewhere earlier on that page you went past a word that you didn't know the meaning of. Either you had no definition for the word or you had an incorrect definition.

Here's an example. "It was found that when the crepuscule arrived the children were quieter and when it was not present they were much more noisy." You see what happens. You think you don't understand the whole idea, but the confusion comes only from one word you didn't know, *crepuscule*, which means the time from sunset to dark.

So you see, the sentence at first looked confusing, but it really only means that the children were quieter at night than they were when the sun was up.

But it isn't just new or hard-looking words that you will have to look up. Some words that are used a lot can often not be understood or wrongly understood and cause confusion. So be sure to look up *any* word that you are not sure of when you are reading this book.

This is the most important thing to know in the whole subject of study. It is the reason that people give up on studying something.

If the book becomes confusing or you can't seem to grasp what you are studying or do what the book is asking you to do, there will be a word just earlier that you have not understood. Don't go any further, but go back to *before* you got into trouble, find the word you did not understand and look it up.

Once you have looked up the word and fully understand it, then read forward in the book from that point. It should now be easy to understand. If it isn't, there is another word that you don't understand. You must find it and get it looked up and fully understood.

Twins

It is best to study this book with another person. This person is called your twin. A **twin** is a person's partner in study. When you have a twin you work together and make sure that you each really understand what you are studying. It makes it easier and more fun.

All through the book there are drills to do. A drill is something that a person does to practice something so that he learns it better. People always need to practice and drill things they want to get really good at.

Do all of the drills with your twin.

If you are reading this book by yourself and do not have a twin, then write down the answers to the drills on a piece of paper or find a person who can listen to you do them out loud. If there is a drill that says to take turns with your twin and you don't have a twin, just do the whole drill yourself.

Drilling will help you a lot!

Contents

CHAPTER ONE:

GRAMMAR

What Is Grammar?

Grammar is the way that spoken words and written words are put together so that thoughts and ideas can go from one person to another.

Some people have taught grammar in a boring or hard way. This has made it seem like a bunch of rules that are not very important and only need to be known so you can pass a test. But it does not have to be boring or hard at all.

Grammar is something that you can learn and **USE** to talk and write so that other people know what you mean. It can also help you to understand better what other people say and write.

This book has been put together so you can learn grammar and become really good at using it in life.

He does not know grammar so he is not understood.

He knows grammar so he can be understood.

The painter does not know grammar.

He got into trouble.

You can see that people who do not know the right way for words to be put together have a lot of trouble in life.

The reason they have trouble is because they can't get other people to understand them.

I DO NOT
UNDERSTAND YOU.

Drill

1. Use a sheet of paper and write down what grammar is and why knowing grammar can help you.

CHAPTER TWO:
COMMUNICATION

Communication

One person can talk to another person and be understood and listen to another person and understand.

What Is Communication?

Here is Jill. She wants to tell Betty that it is good to see her.

Jill is telling Betty, "It is good to see you." Jill is starting the communication. Her communication goes across a distance. Betty is receiving it.

Betty has received and understood the communication. She received it exactly as Jill wanted her to.

They are communicating.

Dear Mom,
I am having fun at camp.
Love,
Hubert
MAIL

They are communicating.

Language is important to communication.

Language is all of the words and the way they are used by people in a country or group.

If you do not understand the communication you receive, no communication and no understanding takes place.

This is true in all kinds of communication. It is true in talking to someone, watching television or movies, reading books, writing letters and so on.

Drill

1. Get an idea and communicate it to your twin.

Communication and Grammar

People use grammar to express themselves. **Express** means to make something known. This can be done by words or actions or pictures.

The better a person knows grammar, the better he can express himself and the more clearly he will be able to understand others and be understood by them.

We use grammar so that we can communicate our ideas to others.

IT IS 5:00.
TOM SAYS IT IS 5:00.

The better you know grammar, the better you can express yourself.

If you know grammar well, you can understand other people and be understood by them.

If you know grammar you can be understood, you can read properly and you can hear properly and if you do not understand grammar you will not be able to.

Drill

1. Use a sheet of paper and write down why grammar can help you to communicate.

CHAPTER THREE:

HOW SPOKEN AND WRITTEN COMMUNICATION BEGAN

How Spoken and Written Communication Began

Knowing how spoken and written communication began will help you understand and use grammar.

We start with an object. It has no name and there is no way to communicate about it except by pointing it out, showing it to someone or drawing it.

People see this thing and want to communicate to each other about it.

It is a little hard to drag one around in order to show it to someone.

There is not always one around to point out and drawing it is not very practical (easy to do).

An answer is to invent a spoken sound that represents this thing. Often the sound that is made is like some sound that is connected with the object.

For example, a flying bat's wings as they strike together, seem to say "bat"—a sound. So now when a person hears the sound "bat" it communicates the idea of this object.

That is the way spoken communication began.

But people sometimes also needed to write down their communication so others could see it. So written symbols were made for these spoken sounds.

A **symbol** is something that can stand for a thought or a thing. An example of a symbol is =. That symbol means *equals*.

A long time ago, people used drawings to show their ideas to others. They would draw a picture of their idea and someone else could look at it and see what they were communicating.

This, for example, is a drawn symbol for the idea *man*. You could see this in cave drawings.

Thousands of years ago, the Egyptians used pictures or drawn symbols to communicate their ideas. These were called *hieroglyphs*. A **hieroglyph** is a picture or symbol that represents (stands for) a word or an idea. Here is an example of an Egyptian hieroglyph for man.

The Chinese used hieroglyphs called **characters** to represent their ideas. The Chinese character for *man* or *person* looked like this:

The trouble with a hieroglyph is that it has to be memorized and it doesn't tell you how to make the spoken sound of it. Chinese has 250,000 of them! This makes it very hard to learn to read and write.

Drill

1. Get an idea and communicate it to your twin using sounds.

Drill

1. Get an idea and communicate it to your twin using symbols.

Many languages which came later used a system that represented sounds with symbols called **letters**.

You could put these letters together and make words which represented ideas and could be used in written communication.

When we want to get the idea of a man across we write M-A-N and other people know what we are talking about.

These letters also represent a certain sound, so when they are all put together (man) it makes one sound which is what everyone who speaks English knows is the spoken word for *man*.

Words are symbols.

Words are used to communicate ideas or thoughts.

Words are not the thing itself.

The word *bat* is a symbol for a bat. It is not a bat itself.

There are many sounds or symbols that have more than one meaning.

Bat can mean several things.

It can mean *a small animal that looks like a mouse with wings and is able to fly.*

BAT

It can also mean *a stick or club used to hit a ball in baseball.*

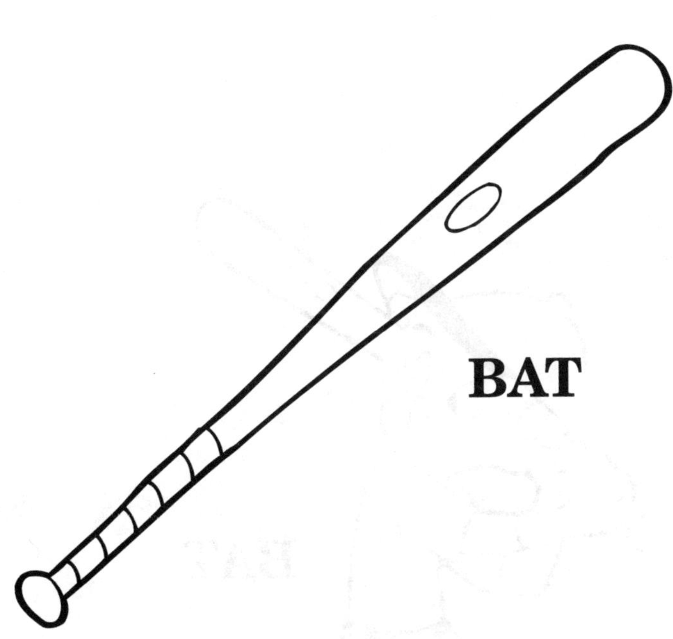

Bat has another meaning which is *to hit a ball with a club or bat.*

So you can see that these three ideas

are all communicated by the same sound or symbol *bat*.

Drill

1. Get an idea and communicate it to your twin using written words.

CHAPTER FOUR:

PARTS OF SPEECH

Parts of Speech

Speech is the communication of thoughts and feelings by spoken words.

You use words in different ways in order to say exactly what you mean.

Words do different things. Some words name things, some words describe things, some words show action. It is sort of like different words do different jobs when they are used with other words. These different jobs are naming things, stating an action, describing things, joining two or more words together, etc.

Box names something. It tells what it is. *Big* would describe the box: *big box.* Or you could say, the *big heavy brown box. Lift* shows an action: *Lift the big heavy brown box.*

These different jobs that words do are called the **parts of speech.**

Understanding the way a word is being used can help you understand the communication that you give and receive.

You are now going to learn the different parts of speech.

Noun

A **noun** is a word that names the things we are talking about. A noun names a person, place or thing.

SALLY
noun

MAN
noun

TEACHER

noun

STUDENTS

noun

ISLAND

noun

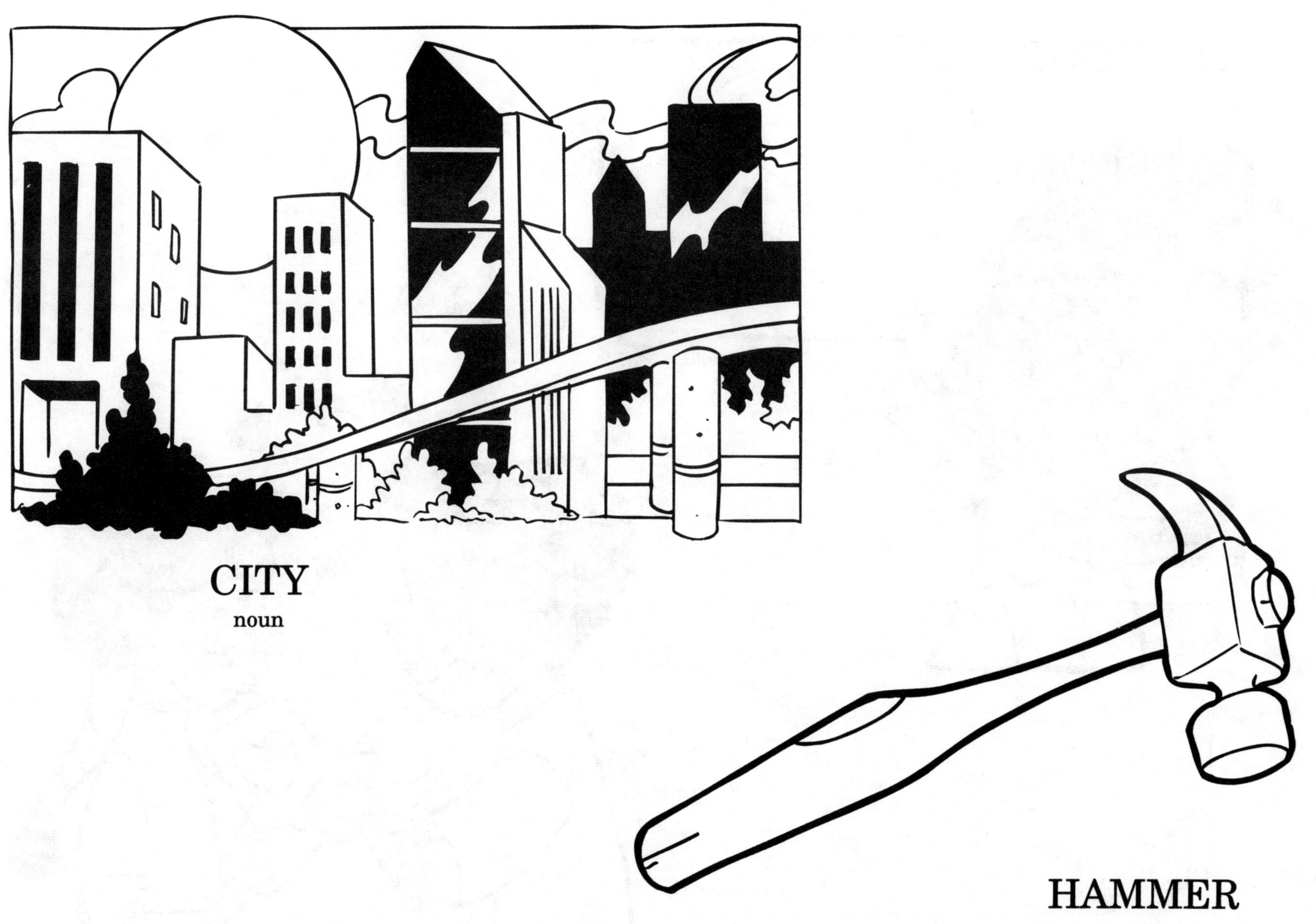

CITY

noun

HAMMER

noun

THOUGHT
noun

LOVE
noun

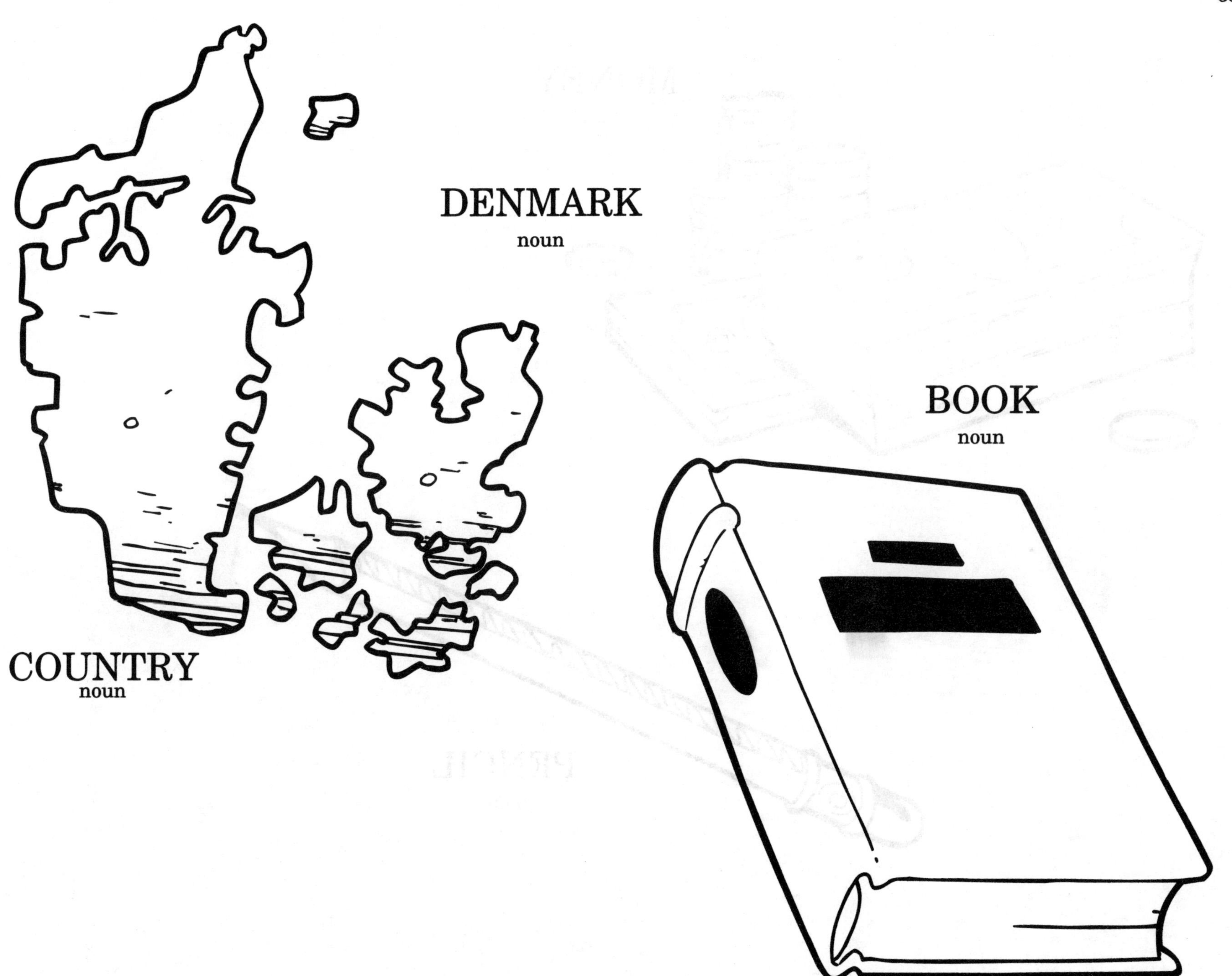
DENMARK
noun
BOOK
noun
COUNTRY
noun

MONEY

noun

PENCIL

noun

Drill

1. Use a sheet of paper and write down ten nouns. Show them to your twin.

Here are some more examples of nouns:

town	tractor	house
friend	plant	basket
mother	store	tree
group	number	cow

These words name things too and they are also nouns.

time	peace	boredom
beauty	happiness	laughter
sadness	helpfulness	fear

Common Noun

A common noun names any person, place or thing in a general class or group.

Proper Noun

A proper noun is the name of a particular person, place or thing. Proper nouns always begin with a capital letter.

THESE ARE CAPITAL LETTERS. These are small letters.

Here are some more examples of common nouns and proper nouns.

Common Noun	**Proper Noun**
president	George Washington
state	New York
girl	Mary Smith
planet	Earth
day	Friday
school	Ramona School
mountain	Mount Everest
month	June

Drills

1. With your twin, walk around the room and point out some things. Tell him the names of the things. These words are nouns.

2. Use a sheet of paper and write down ten examples of common nouns. Show them to your twin.

3. Use a sheet of paper and write down ten examples of proper nouns. Show them to your twin.

4. Use different types of nouns to communicate ideas to your twin until you can see clearly what a noun is and does.

Pronouns

A pronoun is any word that is used in place of a noun.

HE
pronoun

IT
pronoun

SHE
pronoun

HERS
pronoun

YOURS
pronoun

HIS
pronoun

THEIRS
pronoun

THESE
pronoun

THOSE
pronoun

THAT
pronoun

THIS
pronoun

WHO
pronoun
WHAT
pronoun

Drill

1. Use a sheet of paper and write down ten examples of pronouns. Show them to your twin.

Speech would sound strange if we did not use pronouns.

Here is an example of how you would sound if you never used any pronouns:

Paul bought a new book and Paul put the new book where Paul could find the new book easily when Paul wanted to read the new book.

So we say:

Paul bought a new book and **he** put **it** where **he** could find **it** easily when **he** wanted to read **it**.

He and **it** are pronouns. They take the place of nouns. Using pronouns helps a person to get the idea of a noun across without having to use the noun over and over again.

Drill

1. Think of something that happened today and tell your twin about it but do not use any pronouns.

2. Now tell your twin about it and use as many pronouns as you want.

Here are some more examples using pronouns:

SALLY PUT **HERS** ON THE TABLE.

THE PUPPY TOOK **IT** AND RAN AWAY.

HUBERT TOOK **HIS** AND PUT **IT** IN THE CAR.

SALLY TOOK **HER** TO
THE STORE.

Different Kinds of Pronouns

There are pronouns that are used instead of the name of the person speaking,

the person spoken to,

or the person or thing spoken about.

These pronouns are called **personal pronouns**. **Personal** means having to do with person. And the reason they are called personal pronouns is because they have to do with the grammar term **person**. In grammar, **person** means a person, people, thing or things communicated about using specific pronouns.

When you use the pronoun *I*, it shows that you are talking or writing about yourself. In grammar, this is called the **first person.**

When you use the pronoun *you*, it shows that you are talking to another person or thing. In grammar, this is known as the **second person.**

The **third person** indicates the person or thing spoken of. *It* is a pronoun which shows that you are speaking or writing about a thing.

On the following pages you will more clearly see all of the personal pronouns and how they are used.

There are pronouns for both singular and plural.

Singular means one. (Child, bird, box and man are all singular.)

Plural means more than one. (Children, birds, boxes and men are all plural.)

First Person

First person refers to the person speaking.

First Person Singular

(**First person singular** means the person is talking about himself.)

First Person Plural

(**First person plural** means the person is talking about himself and one or more others.)

Drill

1. Use a sheet of paper and write down five examples using first person. Show them to your twin.

Second Person

Second person refers to the person or persons (or even animals or things) spoken to.

Second Person Singular

(**Second person singular** means the person is talking to one other person or thing.)

Second Person Plural

(**Second person plural** means the person is talking to two or more other people or things.)

Drill

1. Use a sheet of paper and write down five examples using second person. Show them to your twin.

Third Person

Third person refers to the person, people, thing or things spoken about.

Third Person Singular

(**Third person singular** means the person is talking about one person or thing.)

He is used when talking about a male.

She is used when talking about a female.

It is used when talking about a thing.

HE IS
STANDING UP.
HIS IS
BROKEN.
THERE IS NO PLACE
FOR HIM TO SIT.

SHE IS
STANDING UP.
HERS IS
BROKEN.
THERE IS NO
PLACE FOR
HER TO SIT.

IT HAS A
BROKEN LEG.
ITS IS BROKEN.
WE CAN'T
USE IT.

Third Person Plural

(**Third person plural** means the person is talking about two or more people or things.)

Third person plural does not change when the person is talking about males, females or things.

THEY HAVE
BROKEN LEGS.
THEIRS
ARE BROKEN.
WE CAN'T
USE THEM.

Drill

1. Use a sheet of paper and write down five examples using third person. Show them to your twin.

These are the personal pronouns:

	Singular	Plural
first person	I, mine, me	we, ours, us
second person	you, yours	you, yours
third person	he, his, him she, hers, her it, its	they, theirs, them

Drills

1. Point out the personal pronouns in the following statements. (Take turns with your twin doing one statement each.)

   a. I hope you will come and see me.

   b. Who was the person we saw you with?

   c. They think you should come with us.

   d. Those books are ours, not theirs.

   e. Did you see him today?

   f. I asked her where she put it.

   g. Did you give them yours or mine?

   h. I told him he could take hers if he wanted it.

2. Use a sheet of paper and write down five examples using personal pronouns. Show them to your twin.

Drill Answers

a. I, you, me

b. we, you

c. They, you, us

d. ours, theirs

e. you, him

f. I, her, she, it

g. you, them, yours, mine

h. I, him, he, hers, he, it

Let's look at the other ways pronouns work.

Pronouns are also used instead of a noun where a person or thing doing the action also receives the action.

For example:

John

himself

John hurt *himself*.

Himself is a pronoun. It is used instead of *John*.

These are called **reflexive pronouns.** **Reflexive** means turning back or bending back. A **reflexive pronoun** is used instead of a noun where the person or thing doing the action also receives the action.

Here are some examples of pronouns used that way:

SHE ASKED **HERSELF** A QUESTION.

THE LITTLE BOY DRESSED **HIMSELF**.

THEY TREATED **THEMSELVES** WITH ICE CREAM.

THE CAT SAT **ITSELF** ON THE CHAIR.

HE WILL KEEP **HIMSELF** WARM.

I ATE THE WHOLE DINNER **MYSELF**.

Here are the reflexive pronouns:

myself

yourself

himself

herself

itself

oneself

ourselves

yourselves

themselves

Drills

1. Point out the reflexive pronouns in the following statements. (Take turns with your twin doing one statement each.)

a. He locked himself out of the house.

b. She stared at herself in the mirror.

c. The children earned money for themselves by raking leaves.

d. Did you hurt yourself when you fell?

2. Use a sheet of paper and write down five examples using reflexive pronouns. Show them to your twin.

Drill Answers

1. a. himself

   b. herself

   c. themselves

   d. yourself

There are pronouns that are used to indicate or show the objects, things or people you are talking about without having to use their name.

For example, you could say, "I want *those*," instead of saying, "I want the *apples*." *Those* takes the place of *apples*.

These are called **demonstrative pronouns. Demonstrative** means showing. Demonstrative pronouns take the place of a noun and help to show the noun that is being talked about.

Those is a pronoun.

Or you could say, "Give *that* to me," instead of saying, "Give the box to me." *That* takes the place of *box*.

That is a pronoun.

Here are more examples:

THESE ARE
THE BEST.
THOSE ARE HOT.

THIS IS MY
NEW BICYCLE.
I LIKE THAT!

The following can be used as demonstrative pronouns:

this

that

these

those

Drills

1. Point out the demonstrative pronouns in the following statements. (Take turns with your twin doing one statement each.)

   a. I will take this but I think those are better.

   b. That is for dinner—you can have these now.

   c. What was that? I think that was an airplane.

   d. These are not the ones I asked for—those are.

2. Use a sheet of paper and write down five examples using demonstrative pronouns. Show them to your twin.

Drill Answers

1. a. this, those

   b. That, these

   c. that, that

   d. These, those

There is another kind of pronoun that can be used in place of a noun when asking a question.

These are called **interrogative pronouns. Interrogative** means asking a question.

WHOSE IS THIS?

WHAT WOULD
YOU LIKE?

The following can be used as interrogative pronouns:

who

whose

what

whom

which

Drills

1. Point out the interrogative pronouns in the following statements. (Take turns with your twin doing one statement each.)

a. Who shall I say is calling?

b. Which comes first?

c. What is the time?

d. Whose is that?

2. Use a sheet of paper and write down five examples of interrogative pronouns. Show them to your twin.

Drill Answers

1. a. Who

   b. Which

   c. What

   d. Whose

Pronouns can also be used when you want to refer to people or things without specifying which person or thing.

These are called **indefinite pronouns.** **Indefinite** means not saying or stating exactly.

SEVERAL CAME.

SOMEONE MISSED THE BUS.

BOTH LIKED IT.

ALL HAD A GOOD TIME.

MANY BROKE.

Here are the most common indefinite pronouns:

all
another
any
anybody
anyone
anything
both
each
either
everybody
everyone
everything
few
many
more
most
much
neither
nobody
one
other
several
some
somebody
someone
such

Drills

1. Point out the indefinite pronouns in the following statements. (Take turns with your twin doing one statement each.)

 a. Few are left.

 b. You take one and I'll take the other.

 c. Several have been seen near here.

 d. Someone told him to sit down.

 e. I don't have any.

 f. I want some too.

2. Use a sheet of paper and write down five examples of indefinite pronouns. Show them to your twin.

Drill Answers

1. a. Few

   b. one, other

   c. Several

   d. Someone

   e. any

   f. some

Some pronouns are used to introduce a group of words which talk about something that was mentioned earlier in the same statement.

These are called **relative pronouns**. **Relative** means related or connected in thought or meaning.

Using relative pronouns lets you communicate what you are saying clearly without having to repeat things so much.

Here is an example:

We found a policeman.

The policeman helped us.

Using a relative pronoun you could say:

We found a policeman *who* helped us.

Here are some more examples of relative pronouns.

Matt is the one *who* won the race.

Football is the sport *which* he likes the best.

This is the car *that* they rented.

She did exactly *what* she was expected to do.

Take the ones *which* are yours, but don't take mine.

Mary is the girl *whom* he met in New York.

When trying to find out what word the relative pronoun refers to, the rule is that the relative pronoun refers to the nearest noun or pronoun in the statement.

The following can be used as relative pronouns :

that

what

which

who

whom

Drills

1. Point out the relative pronouns in the following statements. (Take turns with your twin doing one statement each.)

   a. I met the man that runs the circus and he was very fat.

   b. Lucy saw the people who were supposed to have been there.

   c. They played with a stray dog that had arrived out of nowhere.

   d. She saw the one which was her favorite.

   e. This is very close to what was asked for.

   f. She is the lady whom I saw on TV!

2. Use a sheet of paper and write down five examples of relative pronouns. Show them to your twin.

Drill Answers

1. a. that

   b. who

   c. that

   d. which

   e. what

   f. whom

Verb

A **verb** is a word or words that show action or state of being.

Verbs that show action are words like *running, jumping, skating, screaming*.

State of being means the way that something is or exists. An example of a verb that shows state of being would be *feels* if you said, "She *feels* good." This describes the way that she feels, not something she *is* doing. Another example would be, "He *is* strong."

Here are some examples of verbs that show action:

ROSE **HIT** THE BALL.
verb

MARCO **KICKED** THE BALL.
verb

JOHN **THREW** THE BALL.
verb

BOB **READS** A BOOK.
verb

TOM **WON** A RIBBON.
verb

HE **SEES** A TREE.
verb

SHE **SITS**.
verb

SHE **ATE** THE APPLE
verb

THE TREE **FELL.**
verb

SAM **CUTS** ROSES.
verb

THE FISH **SWIMS**.
verb

THEY **TALK**.
verb

Here are some examples of verbs that show state of being:

ALICE **IS** ANGRY.
verb

BILL **IS** TALL.
verb

THEY **ARE** FRIENDS.
verb

Drill

1. Use a sheet of paper and write down five verbs. Show them to your twin.

TOM AND JANE **DANCED** FOR HOURS.

Danced is a verb. It shows the action that Tom and Jane were doing.

THE GIRL **LOOKED** AT THE PAINTING.

Looked is a verb. It shows the action that the girl was doing.

THE **CHILDREN** ATE THE ICE CREAM.

Ate is a verb. It shows the action that the children were doing.

JUAN **IS** HUNGRY.

Is is a verb. It shows the state of Juan.

THE CHILDREN **ARE** EXCITED.

Are is a verb. It shows the state of the children.

Here are more examples:

THE MEN **WORK** AT THE FACTORY.

SALLY **THOUGHT** ABOUT THE ANSWER.

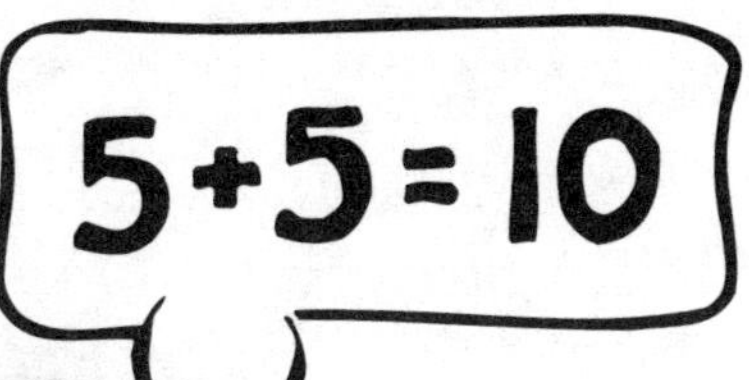

SHE **CAME** HOME YESTERDAY.

THEY **TASTED** THE CAKE.

THE FLOWERS **SMELLED** BEAUTIFUL.

KATHY **IS** HER MOTHER.

THEY **WERE** SAD.

HE **FEELS** HAPPY.

Statements often have more than one verb.

Here are some examples:

John *is* home now and *wants* some food.

She *went* to the party and *danced* all night.

He *ran* to the store, *bought* a new bike and then *rode* it home.

On vacation they *climbed* a mountain, *sailed* a boat and *rode* horses down the beach.

Drills

1. Use a sheet of paper and write down five verbs of action. Show them to your twin.

2. Use a sheet of paper and write down five verbs that show state of being. Show them to your twin.

3. Make up fifteen examples with verbs of action and write them down on a piece of paper. Show them to your twin.

4. Make up fifteen examples with verbs that show state of being and write them down on a piece of paper. Show them to your twin.

5. Point out all the verbs in the following statements. (Take turns with your twin doing one statement each.)

   a. The musicians played for several hours.

   b. We enjoyed the music very much.

   c. They are excellent musicians.

   d. She made chicken for dinner.

   e. It tastes very good.

   f. The noise continued for several minutes and then stopped.

   g. The leaves fell from the tree and covered the ground.

   h. She seems happy with her new gift.

   i. They built the cabin in four days.

   j. They ran far and covered a lot of ground.

Drill Answers

5. a. played

   b. enjoyed

   c. are

   d. made

   e. tastes

   f. continued, stopped

   g. fell, covered

   h. seems

   i. built

   j. ran, covered

A verb is not always a single word.

A verb can be made up of two or more words.

For example, the verb *is* can be used with another verb to show continuing action.

RAMONA **IS PETTING** THE DOG.
verb

FELIPE **IS READING** THE BOOK.
verb

THE FISH **IS SWIMMING**.
verb

SHE **IS SITTING**.
verb

You can see that a verb can be made up of two or more words used to express the action or state of being.

These are called **compound verbs**. **Compound** means made up of two or more parts.

Here are some examples of how this works:

I *go*.

I *will go*.

I *must go*.

I *ate* dinner.

I *will eat* dinner.

I *must eat* dinner.

I *have eaten* dinner.

I *must have eaten* dinner.

I **AM THINKING**.

I **CAN SING**.

WE **WILL BE GOING** TO THE MOVIES TONIGHT.

HE **IS LOOKING** FOR HIS FAVORITE BOOK.

SHE **HAS BEEN CLEANING** HER ROOM.

THEY **WERE PLAYING** BASEBALL.

Drills

1. Tell your twin how many words make up the verb in each statement below. (Take turns with your twin doing one statement each.)

a. The children have gone to school.

b. All of the workmen are eating their lunches.

c. They will be playing at 7:00.

d. The kittens are sleeping.

e. The dog is being washed.

f. It ran up the hill.

g. They liked the dinner.

h. We have finished the job.

i. It should have worked.

2. Make up at least five examples which have compound verbs and write them down on a piece of paper. Show them to your twin.

3. Point out the compound verbs in the following example. (Take turns with your twin doing one statement each.)

When we got to the campground we could see that it had rained. It had rained so hard that the bridge had been washed away. A new bridge was being built where the old one had stood. We decided to turn back and follow the road that would take us to a drier campground.

4. Make up ten more examples using compound verbs and tell them to your twin.

Drill Answers

1. a. have gone—2

   b. are eating—2

   c. will be playing—3

   d. are sleeping—2

   e. is being washed—3

   f. ran —1

   g. liked—1

   h. have finished—2

   i. should have worked—3

3. could see
   had rained
   had rained
   had been washed
   was being built
   had stood
   would take

Verbs and Tense

Verbs express time by changing their form (their sound or spelling). This is called **tense**.

Tense comes from a Latin word meaning *time*. (Latin is the language spoken in and around Rome until about 1,800 years ago.)

Verbs express action or state of being but they also express when the action or state of being occurs.

They express if the action or state of being is in the present *(present tense)*, the past *(past tense)* or the future *(future tense)*.

ELENA **PLAYS** BALL. Present time (present tense)

ELENA **PLAYED** BALL. Past time (past tense)

ELENA **WILL PLAY** BALL. Future time (future tense)

JOHN **LIKES** SKIING. Present time (present tense)

JOHN **LIKED** SKIING. Past time (past tense)

JOHN **WILL LIKE** SKIING. Future time (future tense)

SUZIE **HAS** A BIKE. Present time (present tense)

SUZIE **HAD** A BIKE. Past time (past tense)

SUZIE **WILL HAVE** A BIKE. Future time (future tense)

It is important that you understand tense.

You can be very exact about communicating the idea of what time period you are talking about: past, present or future.

If a person wanted to say that the house burned down, but said instead, "The house will burn down," he not only communicates something that is not true but someone can get the idea that he is planning to burn down the house.

Present Tense

The present tense is used to tell that something exists or is happening at the present moment.

SHE **IS DROPPING** THE PLATES.

Here are more examples:

The kitten *is* on the fence.

These shoes *feel* tight.

Joe *wants* a good book.

I *like* ice cream.

Summer *begins* in June.

Past Tense

The **past tense** is used to tell about something that existed or happened in the past.

Here are more examples:

They *visited* Sweden.

Sam *was* ill.

They *walked* to school.

He *dropped* his book.

She *listened* to music.

Future Tense

The **future tense** is used to tell that something will exist or will happen in the future.

SHE **WILL DROP** THE PLATES.

Here are more examples:

Suzanne *will leave* tomorrow.

In June, my cousin *will visit* me.

Sheila *will be* two years old soon.

It *will get* cold next month.

He *will pay* you five dollars if you *will help* him.

Drills

1. Use a sheet of paper and write down three examples where the verb is in the present tense. Show these to your twin.

2. Use a sheet of paper and write down three examples where the verb is in the past tense. Show these to your twin.

3. Use a sheet of paper and write down three examples where the verb is in the future tense. Show these to your twin.

Sentences

In order to see how verbs and compound verbs and nouns and pronouns are used together to make correct communications, it is necessary to understand what a *sentence* is.

A **sentence** is a group of words put together which expresses a complete thought.

A complete thought is one that tells you something. *The boy* is not a complete thought. It doesn't tell you anything about the boy or what he did. *The boy ran* is a complete thought because it tells you what the boy did. *The boy is big* is also a complete thought.

A sentence must have at least a **subject** and a **verb**. The **subject** of a sentence is the person or thing that is being talked about.

HE SEES THEM.
subject verb

THE **TEA IS** HOT.
subject verb

Sometimes the subject is not stated in the sentence.

STOP!
verb

In the above sentence the subject is understood to be *you*.

(YOU) **STOP**!
subject verb

Here are some more examples of sentences:

THE DOG EATS.
subject verb

SHE LAUGHED.
subject verb

I AM HAPPY.
subject verb

THE **VASE BROKE**.
subject verb

THE **FIRE IS** HOT.
subject verb

WAIT!
verb

(YOU) **WAIT**!
subject verb

Sentences can have two or more sets of subjects and verbs along with other words which say more about the subjects and verbs.

The **plants** **are growing** fast because
subject verb

she **waters** them daily.
subject verb

He **opened** the door for her and **she**
subject verb subject

walked in.
verb

Drills

1. Tell your twin five sentences.

2. Make up five sentences and tell your twin what the subject is in those sentences.

3. Make up five sentences and tell your twin what the verb is in those sentences.

4. Point out the subject and the verb in each of the following sentences. (Take turns with your twin doing one sentence each.)

a. The tree grew.

b. A bird can fly.

c. The clock stopped.

d. She is tall.

e. They ate ice cream.

Drill Answers

4. a. tree (subject), grew (verb)

   b. bird (subject), can fly (verb)

   c. clock (subject), stopped (verb)

   d. She (subject), is (verb)

   e. They (subject), ate (verb)

Transitive Verb

Transitive means *going over or across.*

A **transitive verb** shows action going across to something.

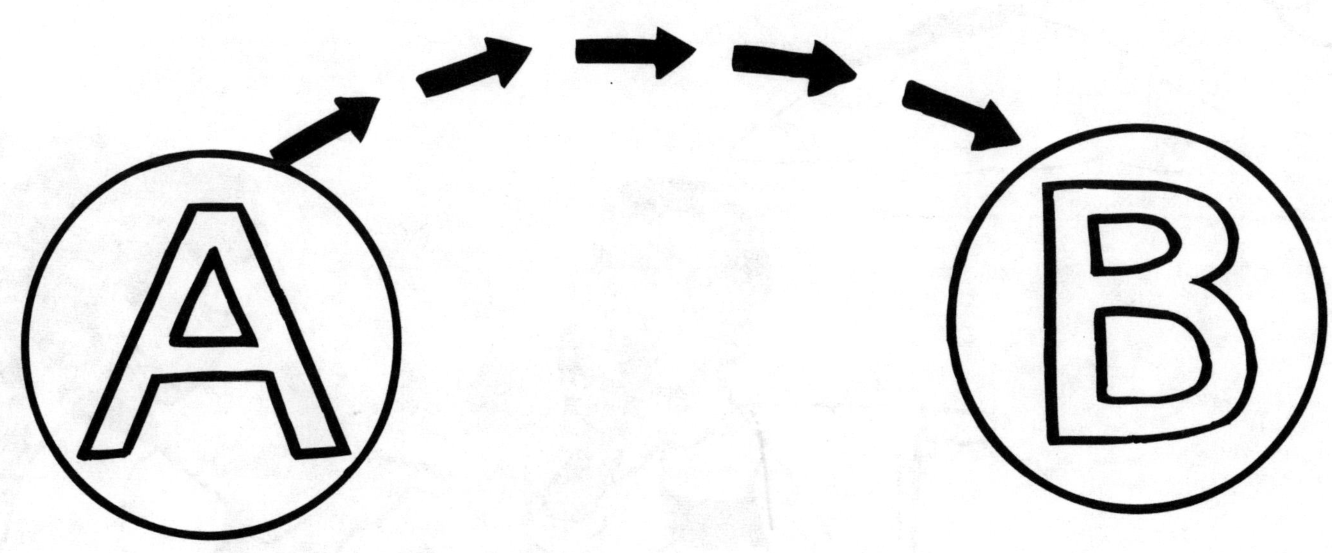

HE **SEES** A TREE.

transitive verb

THEY **ARE PLAYING** CHECKERS.

transitive verb

MIKE **IS READING** A BOOK.
transitive verb

RAMONA **IS PETTING** THE DOG.
transitive verb

KATE **IS WAVING** A FLAG.

transitive verb

SAM **CUTS** ROSES.

transitive verb

SHE **ATE** THE APPLE.
transitive verb

KIM **WON** A RIBBON.
transitive verb

A transitive verb shows the action of the verb going out from someone or something over to someone or something else. With a transitive verb the action directly affects someone or something else.

He ***slammed*** the *door*.

The truck ***pushed*** the little *car* out of the way.

Johnny ***washed*** his *car*.

Alice ***made*** all the party *decorations*.

We ***watched*** a good *movie*.

The thief ***stole*** all the *jewels*.

Intransitive Verb

Intransitive means *not transitive.*

An **intransitive verb** shows action not going across to something.

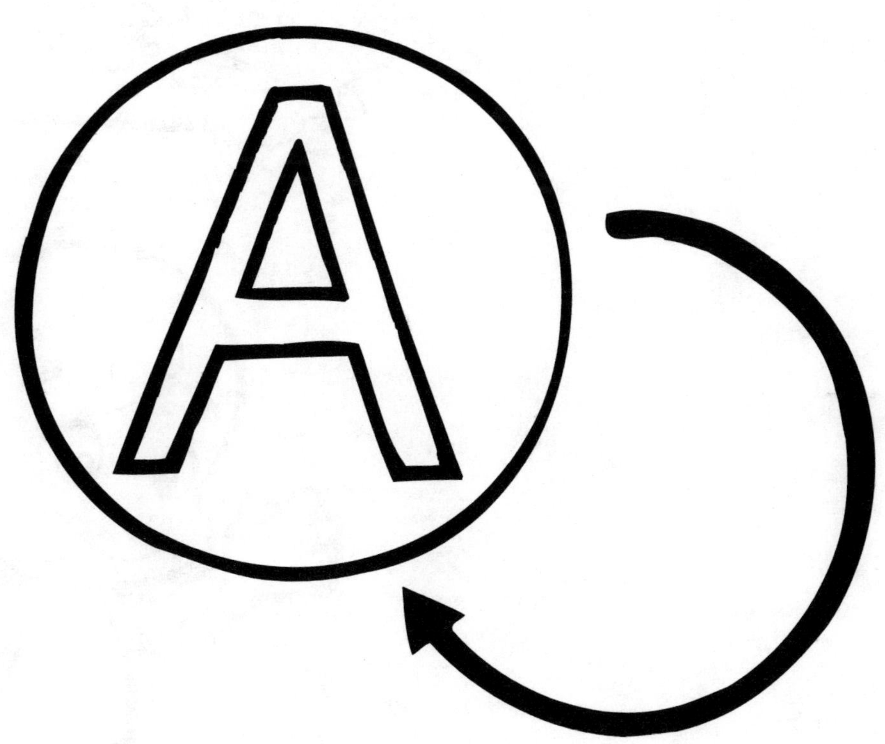

THE FISH **IS SWIMMING.**

intransitive verb

THE BABY **IS WAVING.**

intransitive verb

THE TREE **FELL.**

intransitive verb

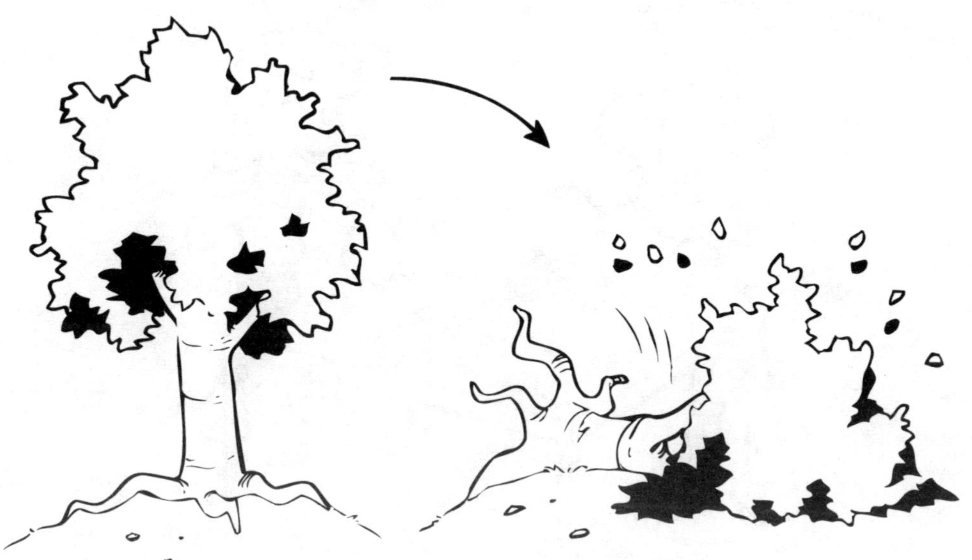

ALEX **WON.**

intransitive verb

SHE **IS SITTING**.

intransitive verb

THEY **ARE PLAYING**.

intransitive verb

THEY **ARE TALKING**.

intransitive verb

With an intransitive verb the action is just done by the subject and the verb does not express that the action goes across to someone or something else.

An intransitive verb can show the action of the verb referring back to the subject of the sentence and is just done by the subject of the sentence without going across to someone else.

The fireman rang the alarm. (transitive)

The alarm rang. (intransitive)

He ***walked*** all day long.

The cat ***is playing***.

The children ***were daydreaming***.

She ***ran*** fast.

Drills

1. Use a sheet of paper and write down ten examples of a transitive verb. Show these to your twin.

2. Use a sheet of paper and write down ten examples of an intransitive verb. Show these to your twin.

Using Transitive and Intransitive Verbs

Most verbs can be used as transitive verbs and intransitive verbs.

You can tell whether they are transitive or intransitive by looking at the rest of the words in the sentence.

He *walked* the dog down the street.

This is transitive. The action is going across from *him* to the dog.

He *walked* down the street.

This is intransitive. The action is not going across to anyone or anything but is done by the subject and the action ends with the subject *(He)*.

The *man* runs a business.

This is transitive because the action of running is going across from the man to the business.

The man *runs* fast.

This is intransitive because the running refers back to the man.

If the action goes across to someone or something else, it is transitive. If the action refers back to the subject and does not go across to someone or something else, it is intransitive.

Verbs which express a state of being rather than an action are always intransitive.

I *feel* great.

She *looks* pretty.

The boys *are thrilled* to be going.

Drill

1. Look at the following sentences and tell your twin whether the verbs are transitive or intransitive. (Take turns with your twin doing one sentence each.)

a. He *melted* the snow in his hands.

b. The snow *melted* in the summer.

c. He *eats* sandwiches for lunch.

d. John *walked* away in a hurry.

e. The movie just *ended*.

f. They just *ended* the game.

g. Annie *laughed* very loudly.

h. The boys *took* the fruit with them.

i. He *opened* his presents really fast.

j. The door *opened* slowly.

Drill Answers

1. a. *melted*—transitive

   b. *melted*—intransitive

   c. *eats*—transitive

   d. *walked*—intransitive

   e. *ended*—intransitive

   f. *ended*—transitive

   g. *laughed*—intransitive

   h. *took*—transitive

   i. *opened*—transitive

   j. *opened*—intransitive

Verbs and Person

Although the subject of *person* has been covered earlier in the section on pronouns, it needs to be explained more fully as it applies to verbs.

In the **first person** it is the person or people *speaking* that do the action described by the verb.

I ***am going*** home.

In this sentence, the person doing the action is *I*, the person speaking. This is called the *first person* and the verb *am going* is said to be in the first person.

We ***are going*** home.

This is also the *first person*. The person or people speaking are doing the action described by the verb.

In the **second person** it is the person or people *spoken to* that do the action described by the verb.

You ***are going*** home.

In the **third person** it is the person, people, thing or things *spoken about* that do the action described by the verb.

He ***is going*** home.
Joe is ***going*** home.

She ***is going*** home.
My *sister* ***is going*** home.

It ***is going*** home.
The *dog* ***is going*** home.

They ***are going*** home.
The cars ***are going*** home.

Person is also divided into singular (one person or thing) and plural (more than one person or thing).

I ***am going*** home. (one person)
This is first person singular.

We ***are going*** home. (more than one person)
This is first person plural.

Here is the present tense of the verb *go.*

	Singular	Plural
first person	I **go**	we **go**
second person	you **go**	you **go**
third person	he **goes** she **goes** it **goes**	they **go**

As you can see, the verb endings change in some cases to show *person*. The third person singular of *go (goes)* is different from the first person singular *(go)*.

Here is the present tense of the verb *talk*.

	Singular	**Plural**
first person	I **talk**	we **talk**
second person	you **talk**	you **talk**
third person	he **talks** she **talks** it **talks**	they **talk**

Here is the present tense of the verb *be*.

	Singular	Plural
first person	I **am**	we **are**
second person	you **are**	you **are**
third person	he **is** she **is** it **is**	they **are**

Drill

1. In the following sentences point out which person each of the verbs is in and whether it is singular or plural. (Take turns with your twin doing one statement each.)

a. She often *goes* out with the boys.

b. I *love* watching the surf crash on the rocks.

c. They often *get* home late.

d. It looks like he *fell* down the hill.

e. You dogs must *remain* here.

f. Do you *live* here?

Drill Answers

1. a. third person singular

   b. first person singular

   c. third person plural

   d. third person singular

   e. second person plural

   f. second person singular

Agreement

When putting together sentences, the verbs you use have to "agree" with the subject (person or thing) they are talking about.

If the subject and verb of a sentence don't agree, the sentence won't communicate clearly.

For example, you wouldn't say, "I goes home." *I* is first person singular, so you would have to say, "I go home."

You wouldn't say, "They is stupid." You would say, "They are stupid."

You wouldn't say, "The man go fast." You would say, "The man goes fast."

That is *agreement* between the subject and verb. That is all agreement means.

For a verb to agree with the subject it must be the same *number. Number* simply refers to if it is singular or plural.

I is singular, *we* is plural. If the subject of a sentence is singular (talking about one person, for example *I*) then the verb of that sentence must be singular. It must agree in number.

(first person singular)

(second person singular)

(third person singular)

(first person plural)

(second person plural)

(third person plural)

For a verb to agree with the subject it must also be in the same *person* (first person, second person, third person) as the subject. If the subject of the sentence is in the second person (i.e., *you*) then the verb of that sentence must also be in the second person. It must agree in person.

I am here.
(first person singular)

You ***are*** here.
(second person singular)

He (she or it) ***is*** here.
(third person singular)

We ***are*** here.
(first person plural)

You ***are*** here.
(second person plural)

They ***are*** here.
(third person plural)

If the verb does not agree with the thing or person it is talking about, it will sound strange and it will not communicate.

Drills

1. Point out where the verbs in the following sentences do not agree with the subjects either in number or person and tell your twin what the verb should be so that it would agree. (Take turns with your twin, doing one sentence each.)

a. He are coming soon.

b. They is coming soon.

c. They goes to the theater every Wednesday.

d. When I is ready, I will go.

2. Get a simple idea and communicate it to your twin using a subject and a verb that do not agree. Then communicate it using a subject and a verb that do agree.

Drill Answers

1. a. He *is* coming soon.

   b. They *are* coming soon.

   c. They *go* to the theater every Wednesday.

   d. When I *am* ready, I will go.

The Different Forms of a Verb

Verbs have different forms, as you have seen. **Forms** refers to the different ways that the verbs are spelled and spoken.

By learning the correct forms of verbs you can express different things with the verbs. You can say, "I run" or "I ran" or "He runs," etc.

Putting together the different forms of a verb in their correct order is called **conjugation**. By studying a verb's conjugation, you can learn the correct forms of a verb. You will then know the correct way to use them when you write and speak.

Like is a regular verb.

Regular verbs are called regular because their past form is made by adding *ed* or *d*.

Seeing the conjugation of a simple regular verb will help you understand all the different forms of the verb and you will be able to apply this to other regular verbs.

For example, if you saw the word *talks*, you would know that it is a form of *talk* and would be in the dictionary under *talk*.

On the following pages the verb *like* is conjugated to show you some of its forms.

LIKE

Present Tense

	Singular	Plural
first person	I **like**	we **like**
second person	you **like**	you **like**
third person	he **likes** she **likes** it **likes**	they **like**

LIKE

Past Tense

	Singular	Plural
first person	I **liked**	we **liked**
second person	you **liked**	you **liked**
third person	he **liked** she **liked** it **liked**	they **liked**

LIKE

Future Tense

	Singular	Plural
first person	I **will like**	we **will like**
second person	you **will like**	you **will like**
third person	he **will like** she **will like** it **will like**	they **will like**

The endings of regular verbs will be the same from verb to verb.

Here are some more examples.

enjoy
enjoys
enjoyed

laugh
laughs
laughed

paint
paints
painted

walk
walks
walked

bake
bakes
baked

Drill

1. Use a sheet of paper and write down ten examples of regular verbs. Show them to your twin.

Verbs are either regular, which means that their past form is made by adding *ed* or *d* to the verb (such as *play, played*) or irregular, which means their past form is made in some other way (such as *sing, sang*).

The endings of an irregular verb will be different from verb to verb and that is what makes the difference between regular and irregular verbs.

Irregular Verbs

be
is
was

run
runs
ran

Be is an irregular verb and its form changes quite a lot. On the following pages are some of the tenses and forms of *be* which show how it is used correctly. This is an example of the conjugation of an irregular verb.

BE

Present Tense

	Singular	Plural
first person	I **am**	we **are**
second person	you **are**	you **are**
third person	he **is** she **is** it **is**	they **are**

BE

Past Tense

	Singular	Plural
first person	I **was**	we **were**
second person	you **were**	you **were**
third person	he **was** she **was** it **was**	they **were**

BE

Future Tense

	Singular	Plural
first person	I **will be**	we **will be**
second person	you **will be**	you **will be**
third person	he **will be** she **will be** it **will be**	they **will be**

Here are some more examples of irregular verbs.

go goes went	sit sits sat
swim swims swam	take takes took
eat eats ate	sing sings sang

Drill

1. Use a sheet of paper and write down ten examples of irregular verbs. Show them to your twin.

If you are not sure of the forms of an irregular verb you can look in a dictionary. Dictionaries usually tell you the forms of a verb.

Drills

1. Point out which of the following verbs are regular and which are irregular. (Take turns with your twin doing one verb each.)

   a. want (past tense—wanted)

   b. seem (past tense—seemed)

   c. eat (past tense—ate)

   d. walk (past tense—walked)

   e. swing (past tense—swung)

   f. see (past tense—saw)

   g. make (past tense—made)

   h. enter (past tense—entered)

2. Take the verb *open* and break it down into its forms (conjugate it) as was done with the verbs *like* and *be*. Write these down on a piece of paper and show them to your twin. Make sure you include past, present and future, singular and plural, first person, second person and third person. You may use a dictionary if you like.

3. Now do the same (repeat drill number 2) for the verb *see*.

Drill Answers

1. a. regular

   b. regular

   c. irregular

   d. regular

   e. irregular

   f. irregular

   g. irregular

   h. regular

Modifiers

A **modifier** is something that describes.

GIRL

LITTLE GIRL
modifier

TALL GIRL
modifier

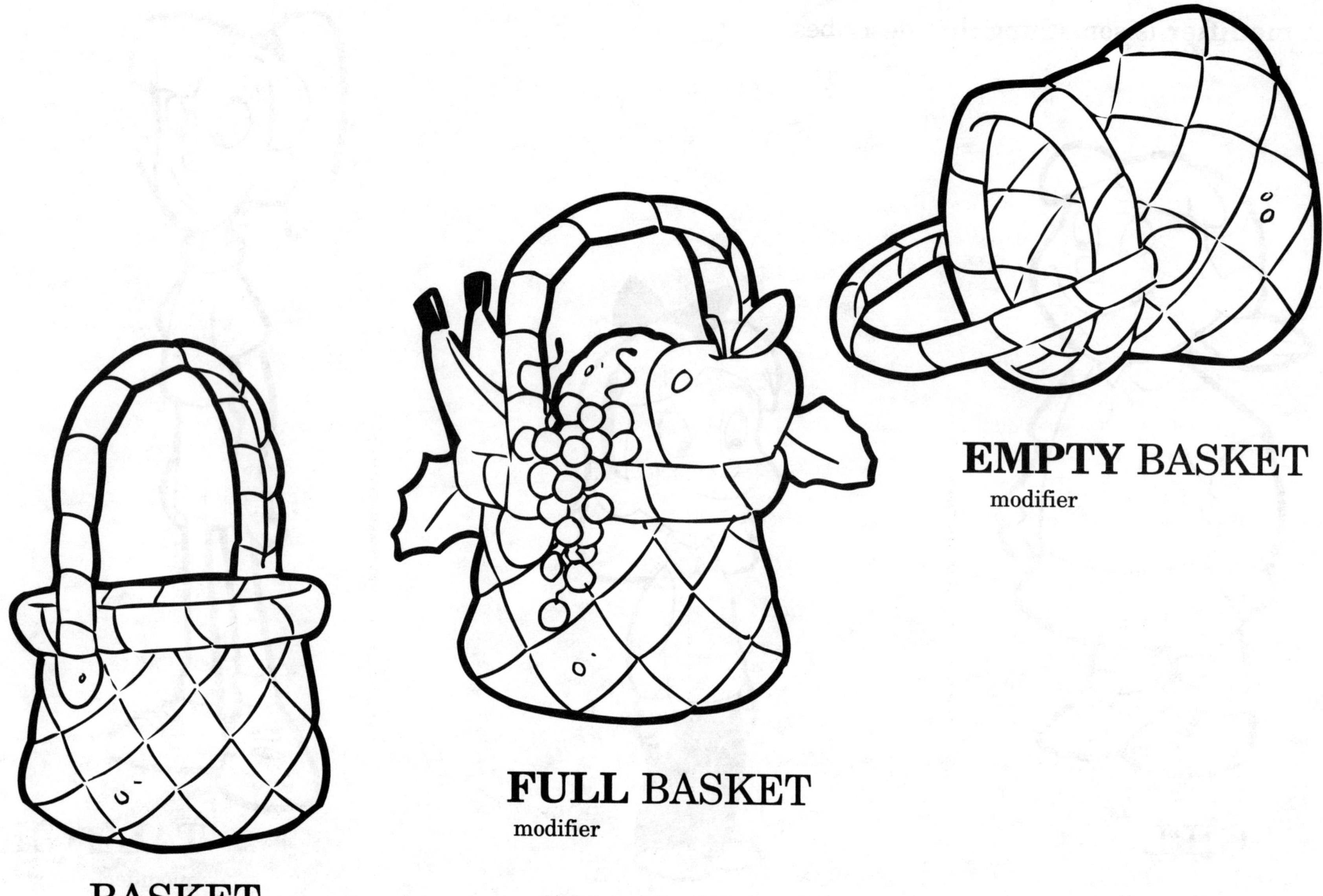
EMPTY BASKET
modifier
FULL BASKET
modifier
BASKET

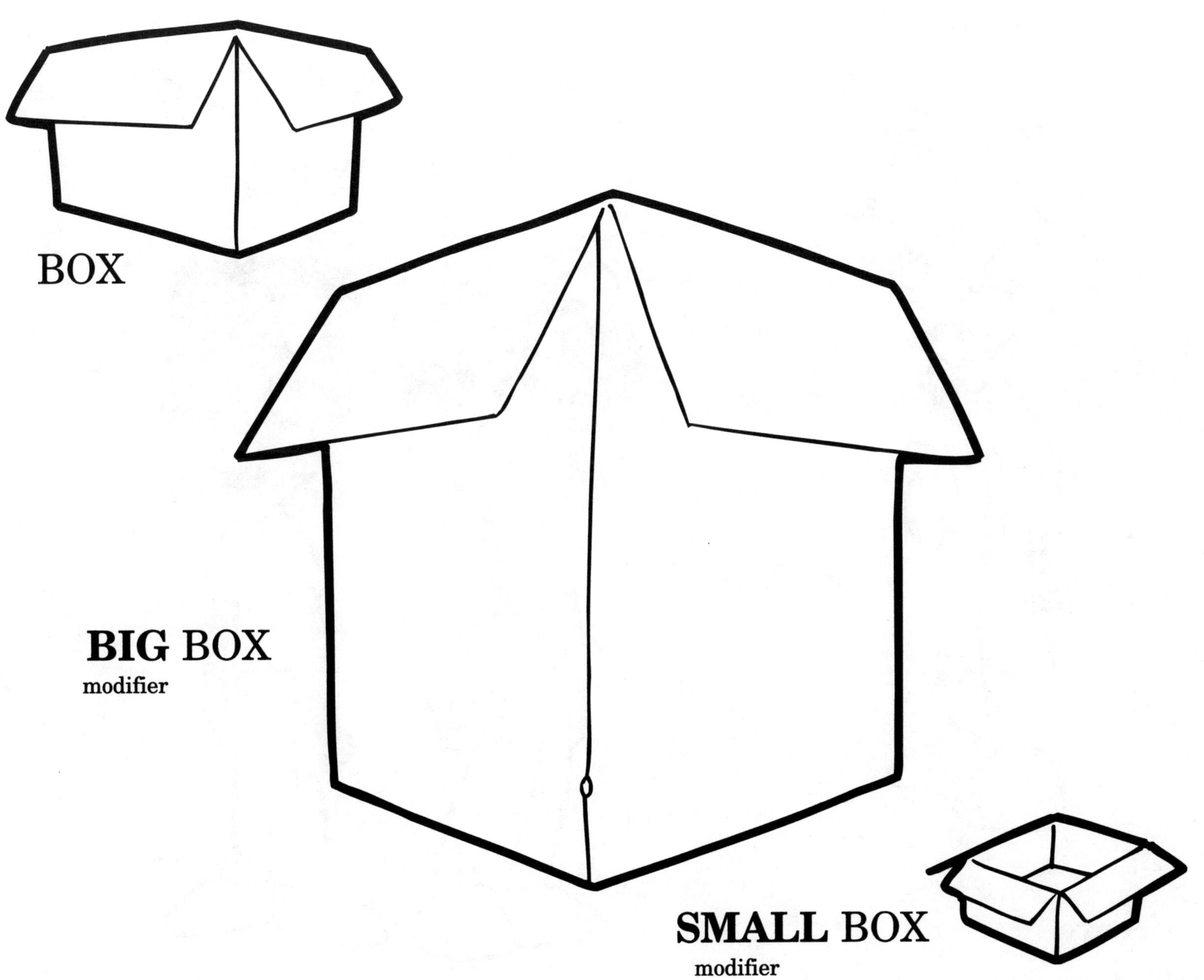
BOX
BIG BOX
modifier
SMALL BOX
modifier

BOY

TWO BOYS
modifier

MANY BOYS
modifier

SHE IS LOOKING.

SHE IS LOOKING **DOWN**.
modifier

SHE IS LOOKING **UP**.
modifier

IT IS **BIG.**

modifier

IT IS **VERY BIG**.
modifier modifier

THE RADIO IS PLAYING **LOUDLY**.
modifier

THE RADIO IS PLAYING **TOO LOUDLY**.

modifier modifier

Drill

1. Use a sheet of paper and write down ten examples of modifiers. Show them to your twin.

You can take a word like *shirt* and by using modifiers to describe it, you can change it quite a lot without changing the fact that you are still talking about a shirt.

ONE SHIRT

THIS WORN-OUT SHIRT

STRIPED SHIRT

BRIGHT SHIRT

EXPENSIVE SILK SHIRT
$100
HEAVY WOOLEN SHIRT

You can take an action like *walking* and by using modifiers you can describe a lot of different things about walking.

WALKING **QUIETLY**

WALKING **LIGHTLY**

WALKING **QUICKLY**
WALKING **SLOWLY**

Modifiers help a person express exactly what he wants to say or write.

For example, you could tell a person that you saw a bus, but you would not be able to get across the idea that it was broken-down unless you used modifiers.

You could tell a person that you saw a boy running but you would not be able to communicate that the boy was running quickly or lazily or sneakily or loudly unless you used modifiers.

Communication would be pretty boring without modifiers!

Drills

1. Find an object in the room and use as many modifiers as you can think of to describe it.

2. Try to describe something to your twin without using any modifiers.

3. Tell your twin a simple, short fairy tale or story or joke but do not use *any* modifiers.

4. Now tell your twin a simple, short fairy tale or story or joke, using as many modifiers as you can.

Modifiers tell one or more things about other words. In the following examples you can see how they are used to modify people, places or things.

When you look in a dictionary or in an older grammar book you will find these kinds of modifiers are called *adjectives*. These are the ones that modify people, places or things.

Which one?

This cat's name is Harriet.
I see *those* boys.
I live in the *yellow* house.

What kind?

Bill was wearing a *heavy* coat.
She made some *pink* lemonade.
I want a *chocolate* one.

How many?

Some cities are very large.
Many stories were told.
Two children watched us.

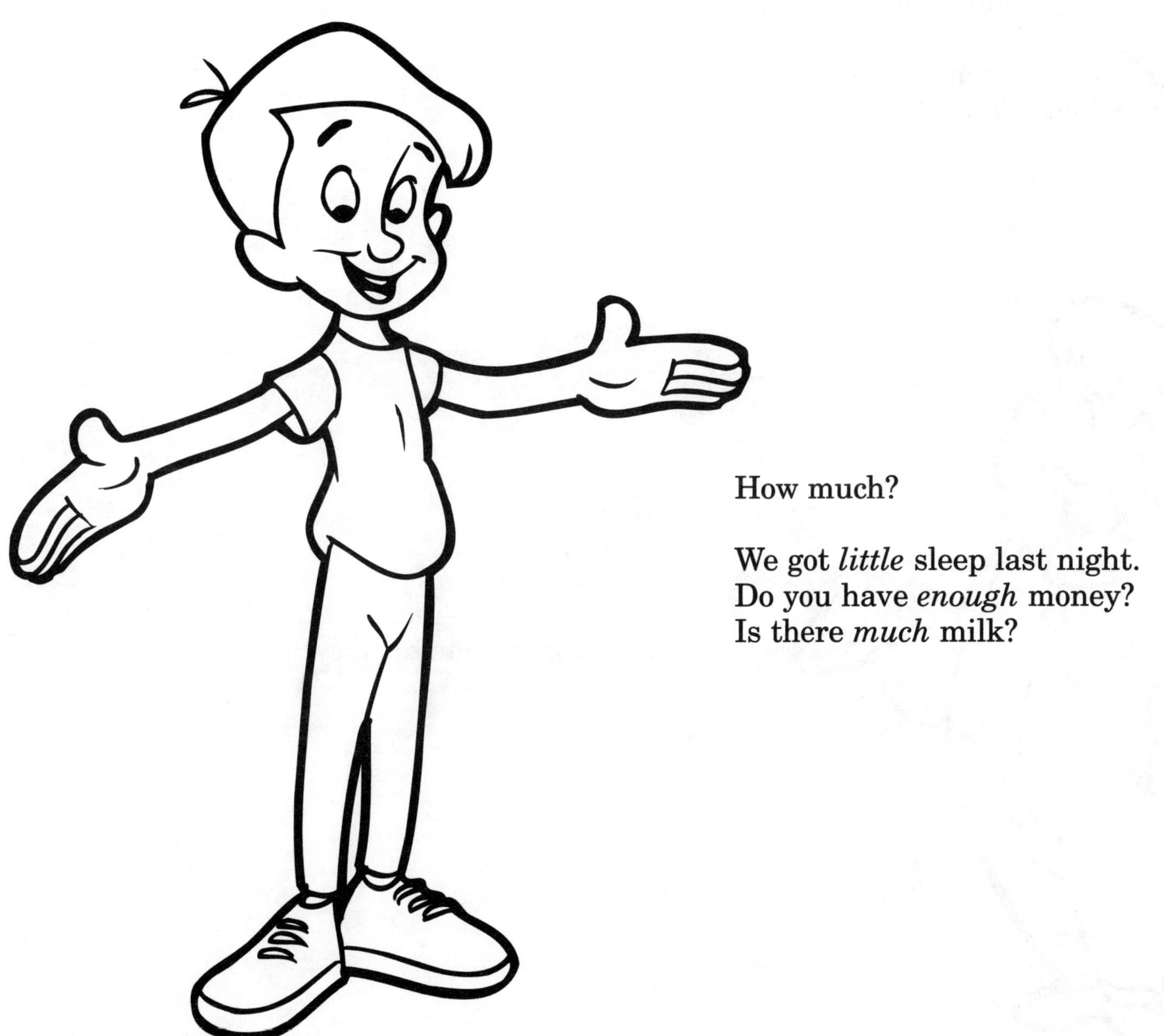

How much?

We got *little* sleep last night.
Do you have *enough* money?
Is there *much* milk?

In the examples below, you can see how modifiers describe things about action.

In dictionaries and older grammar books these modifiers are called *adverbs*.

How?

She answered *angrily*.
The song was sung *beautifully*.
He *happily* rode his bicycle.

When?

They danced *yesterday*.
Father will be home *soon*.
The bus came *late*.

Where?

I walked *there*.
They were playing *outdoors*.
The beach is *near*.

Modifiers can also modify other modifiers.

Here are some examples:

It was an *enjoyable* party.
It was a *most* enjoyable party.

She was *quiet*.
She was *very* quiet.

Here are more examples:

The show was *over*.
The show was *almost* over.

She liked the *red* dress.
She liked the *bright* red dress.

(Modifiers that modify other modifiers would be called adverbs in older grammar books.)

Drills

1. Have your twin tell you a subject and a verb. Finish the sentence by adding a modifier to describe the action.

2. Now take the sentence you have just made and see if you can find a modifier to modify the first modifier you thought of.

3. Repeat 1 and 2 above until you can do it easily.

4. Have your twin tell you a noun. Now think of a modifier for that noun and tell it to your twin. Now think of a modifier to modify the first modifier you thought of.

5. Repeat 4 above until you can do it easily.

6. Tell your twin a modifier. Now think of a modifier to modify that modifier. Use the modifiers in a sentence.

7. Repeat 6 above until you can do it easily.

8. Think of an action and communicate it to your twin using a verb. Now describe it more exactly by using modifiers. See how exactly you can describe your idea. Make sure your twin gets the idea you thought of.

9. Think of an object and describe it to your twin. Now describe it even more exactly by using modifiers. See how exactly you can describe the object. Make sure your twin really gets the idea you thought of.

Article

An **article** is a special kind of modifier. It tells you if the speaker or writer is talking about a specific person, place or thing or whether he is talking about any one person, place or thing out of a general group.

I NEED **A** BOX.

article

I NEED **THE** SMALL BOX.
article

I WANT **AN** APPLE.
article

Indefinite Article

An **indefinite article** is a word used to talk about one thing without pointing it out. It is not definite. That is why it is called *indefinite*.

A and *an* are the indefinite articles.

an apple

an alligator

an elephant

an empty box

an island

an igloo

an octopus

an owl

an umbrella

an ugly spider

an hour

an oak tree

a boat

a coat

a dolphin

a flower

a gorilla

a house

a joke

a letter

a monkey

a potato

a rose

a big turtle

A and *an* do not tell you which. They show you are talking about any one of the kind of things you are referring to.

I bought *a* magazine.

He would like *an* ice cream.

Joe gave me *a* pen.

We saw *a* movie.

Definite Article

A **definite article** is a word used to indicate specific people or things.

The is the definite article.

The flowers smell sweet.

Joe is playing with *the* dog.

I saw *the* children.

The photographs have been developed.

The teacher smiled at him.

The word *tree* just means tree.

A tree refers to any tree out of a lot of trees.

The tree refers to a specific tree.

A blanket refers to any blanket out of a lot of blankets.

The blanket refers to a specific blanket.

Drills

1. Have a short conversation with your twin, using no articles.

2. Use a sheet of paper and write down ten examples using indefinite articles. Show them to your twin.

3. Use a sheet of paper and write down ten examples using the definite article. Show them to your twin.

4. Have another short conversation with your twin, using articles as often as you wish. Notice how frequently they are used.

Preposition

A **preposition** is a word that shows the relationship between a person, place or thing and some other word (or words) in the sentence.

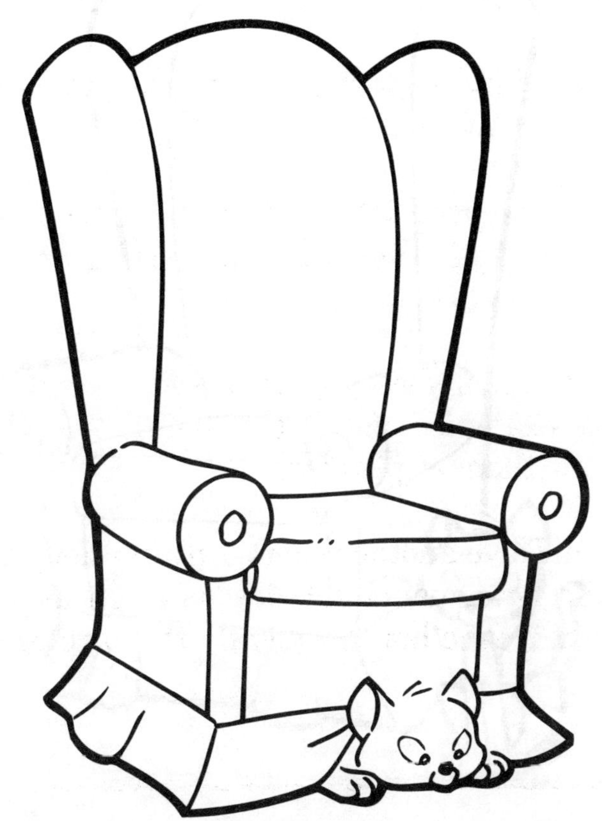

TIGER IS SITTING **UNDER** THE CHAIR.
preposition

TIGER IS SITTING **ON** THE CHAIR.
preposition

TIGER IS SITTING **BY** THE CHAIR.
preposition

TIGER IS SITTING **BEHIND** THE CHAIR.
preposition

MICHELLE IS RUNNING **UP** THE HILL.
preposition

MICHELLE IS RUNNING **DOWN** THE HILL.
preposition

MICHELLE IS **NEAR** THE HILL.
preposition

A BALL IS COMING **OVER** THE NET.

preposition

A BALL IS COMING **AROUND** THE NET.

preposition

A BALL IS COMING **INTO** THE NET.
preposition

Drill

1. Use a sheet of paper and write down ten examples of prepositions. Show them to your twin.

Here are some more examples of prepositions:

Here is a letter *from* your mother.

From shows the relationship between *letter* and *mother*. The letter is *from* mother, not *to* mother or *for* mother.

They walked *across* the street.

Across shows the relationship between *walked* and *street*. They walked *across* the street, not *toward* the street or *away from* the street.

Their house is *near* Miami Beach.

Near shows the relationship between *house* and *Miami Beach*. The house is *near* Miami Beach, not *on* it or *toward* it.

We drove there *after* the movie.

After shows the relationship between *drove* and *movie*. We drove there *after* the movie, not *during* the movie or *before* the movie.

Here are other examples of sentences that have prepositions in them:

This gift is *for* you.

The cat is hiding *under* the bed.

We will not see him *until* next week.

The child walked *behind* his parents.

The water went *down* the drain.

The bow fell *under* the chair.

She sat *between* her brothers.

Don't mistake a modifier for a preposition. Sometimes they can look pretty similar.

Out, for instance, can be a modifier *or* a preposition.

She ran *out* the door.

In this example, *out* is a preposition because it shows the relationship between her running and the door.

She ran *out*.

In this example, *out* is a modifier. It tells where she ran.

The ball fell *down* the hole.

In this example, *down* is a preposition because it shows the relationship between the ball falling and the hole.

The ball fell *down*.

In this example, *down* is a modifier. It tells where the ball fell.

Drills

1. Tell your twin ten sentences that have prepositions in them.

2. Point out the prepositions in the following sentences. (Take turns with your twin doing one sentence each.)

a. The money was left lying in the street.

b. We will get to New York soon.

c. She left her books in her room.

d. Here is a letter from Joe.

e. He is waiting by the door.

f. She is carrying her package under her arm.

g. He leaned his bicycle against the wall.

h. They are from England.

i. I will get it for you.

j. The bird flew over his head.

k. He is coming with his father.

l. They will be here by sunset.

m. He asked the coach if he could play with the team.

Drill Answers

2. a. in

   b. to

   c. in

   d. from

   e. by

   f. under

   g. against

   h. from

   i. for

   j. over

   k. with

   l. by

   m. with

Conjunctions

A **conjunction** is a word or words which join words or groups of words.

AMY **AND** ANITA ARE CARRYING A BOX.
conjunction

ANITA SEES A BOOT **AND** A TABLE **AND** A CUP.

conjunction conjunction

WE CAN PLAY BALL **OR** SWIM.

conjunction

BILL IS TALLER **BUT** MIKE IS HEAVIER.

conjunction

Drill

1. Use a sheet of paper and write down ten examples using conjunctions. Show them to your twin.

And is a conjunction.

SALLY **AND** JUDY LOVE TO GO SHOPPING.

And connects *Sally* and *Judy*. *And* is a conjunction.

The conjunction *and* is used to connect the parts of the sentence and make them into a whole idea.

Here are more examples:

MIKE **AND** TOM WENT TO TOWN.

MIKE, JUDY **AND** JOE ATE PIZZA.

CATS **AND** DOGS FIGHT.

SHE HAD DINNER, TOOK A BATH **AND** WENT TO BED.

But is also a conjunction.

Yesterday it rained *but* today is sunny.

But shows there is a difference between yesterday and today and connects the two ideas.

Here are more examples:

I LOVE CAKE **BUT** HE LIKES ICE CREAM.

SHE GOES TO SLEEP EARLY **BUT** HE GOES TO SLEEP LATE.

I WOULD LOVE TO GO **BUT** I HAVE TO DO MY HOMEWORK.

THE CAT WAS HAPPY **BUT** THE BIRD LOOKED SCARED.

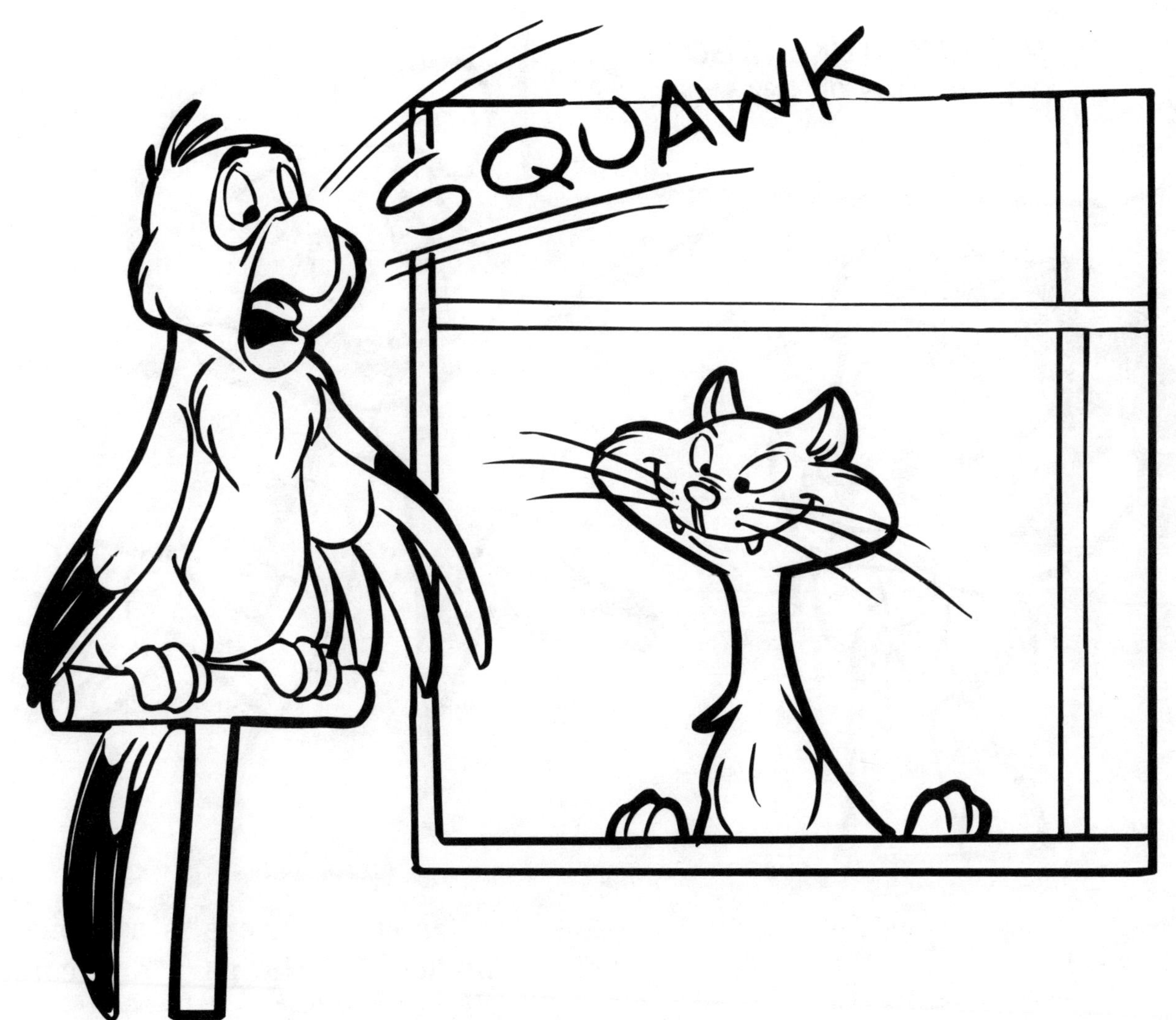

Or is a conjunction:

WOULD YOU LIKE TO GO TO THE MOVIES **OR** THE PARK?

Or shows there is a choice between the movies and the park and connects the two ideas.

Here are more examples:

WILL YOU HAVE PIZZA **OR** HAMBURGERS?

I CAN DO THIS TODAY **OR** TOMORROW.

IS IT RAINY **OR** SUNNY?

WOULD YOU LIKE TO DANCE WITH TOM **OR** JOE?

Here are some more examples of words used as conjunctions:

I will go *if* he goes too.

You can go *when* you have eaten your dinner.

I will do this *while* you do that.

Is the show now *or* later?

You can play *but* only outside.

I will read *while* you draw a picture.

I ate more *than* she ate.

We will go *unless* it rains.

Sometimes conjunctions are used in pairs. Here are some examples of conjunctions used in pairs.

Bring *not only* your bathing suit *but also* your towel.

We ate *both* a turkey *and* a ham.

I will do *either* the dishes *or* the dusting.

Sometimes a conjunction is a group of words, not just one word. The group of words is used to join other words or groups of words.

I will be there *as soon as* I am ready.

I will go *as long as* you go too.

Drills

1. Have a short conversation with your twin using no conjunctions.

2. Tell your twin anything you would like to say, using conjunctions as much as you like.

3. Use a sheet of paper and write down some simple sentences. Then write some longer ones using conjunctions. Do this until you see when and how conjunctions are used.

Interjection

An **interjection** is a word or group of words that show strong feeling.

HELP! I AM FALLING.
interjection

WOW! THAT IS BEAUTIFUL.
interjection

Drill

1. Use a sheet of paper and write down ten examples using interjections. Show them to your twin.

Here are some more examples of interjections:

Ha! I caught you.

Great! I would love to see the movie.

Wow! I just had an idea.

Ouch! I hit my finger.

Good grief! How long have you been here?

We did it. *Hooray!*

There it is! *Oh,* isn't it beautiful!

Drill

1. Use interjections to get the following ideas across to your twin:

a. surprise

b. anger

c. fear

d. sadness

e. excitement

Summary—Parts of Speech

Those are the parts of speech. Here is a list of them.

Noun
Pronoun
Verb
Modifier
Article
Preposition
Conjunction
Interjection

Knowing the parts of speech will help you to understand which definition of a word is being used when you read or hear the word.

If you know the parts of speech well you can express yourself well so that others can understand you and you won't get tongue-tied (unable to talk) or stammer and find it difficult to communicate your ideas.

For this reason the next thing you will do is some more drills on the parts of speech.

Parts of Speech Drills

1. Tell your twin what a noun is. Write down ten nouns. Now use each of the nouns you have written down in a sentence.

2. Tell your twin what a pronoun is. Write down ten pronouns. Now use each of the pronouns you have written down in a sentence.

3. Tell your twin what a verb is. Write down ten verbs. Now use each of the verbs you have written down in a sentence.

4. Now use each of the verbs you just wrote down in another sentence, using a different tense than the one you used before.

5. Tell your twin what a modifier is. Write down ten modifiers. Now use each of the modifiers you have written down in a sentence.

6. Tell your twin what an article is. Write down the articles. Now use each of the articles in three sentences.

7. Tell your twin what a preposition is. Write down ten prepositions. Now use each of the prepositions you have written down in a sentence.

8. Tell your twin what a conjunction is. Write down ten conjunctions. Now use each of the conjunctions you have written down in a sentence.

9. Tell your twin what an interjection is. Write down ten interjections. Now use each of the interjections you have written down in a sentence.

Words That Have More Than One Meaning

Earlier you learned that a sound or symbol can have several meanings. When more than one idea is expressed by a sound or symbol, it is called a **homonym**.

Bat is a homonym.

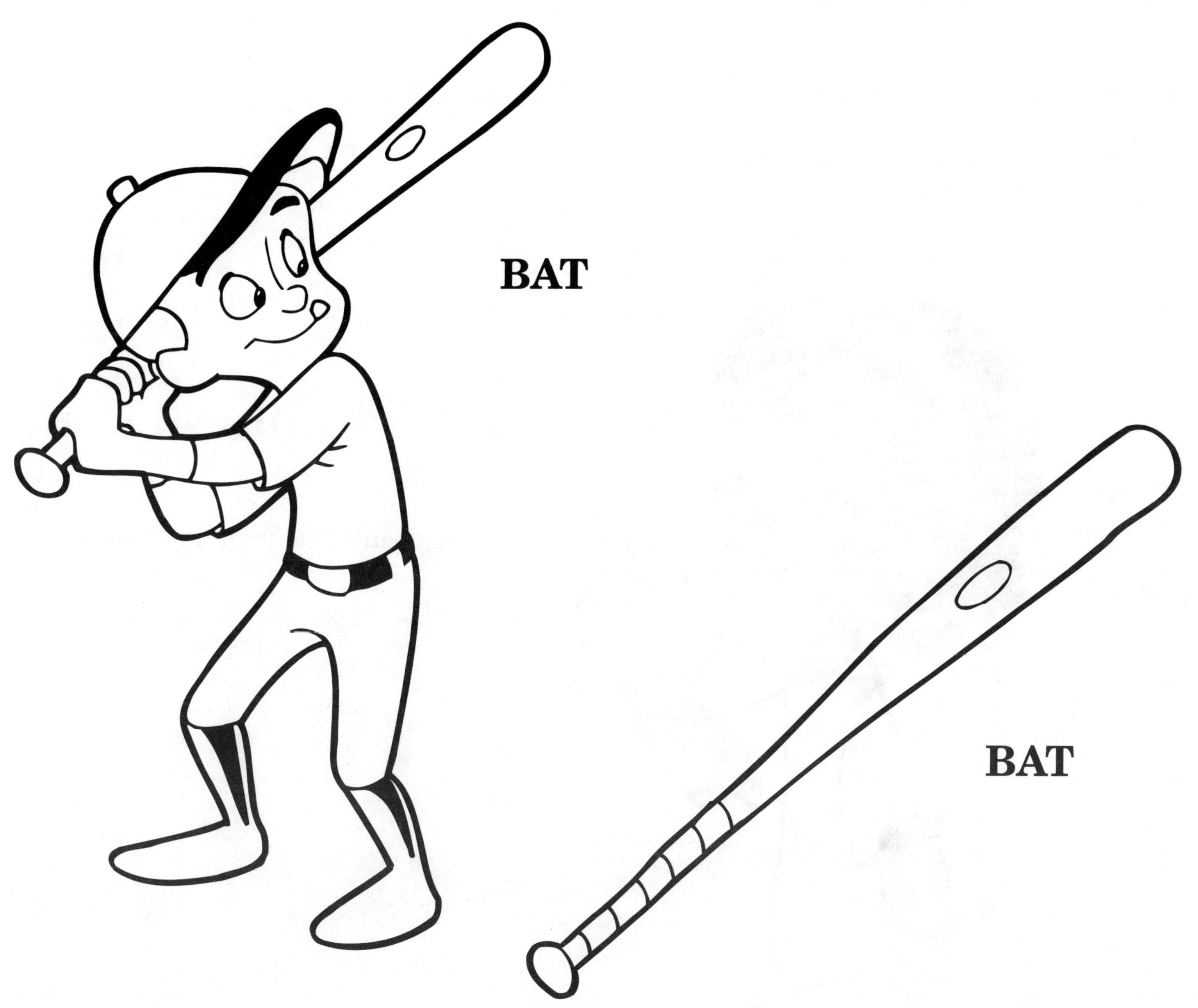
BAT
BAT

Homonyms can be different parts of speech.

An example is the word *drink*.

Drink means to take liquid into the stomach, which is a verb.

SHE HAS TO **DRINK** HER MILK.

In this sentence *drink* is a verb.

Drink is also a beverage.

GIVE ME A **DRINK**.

In this sentence *drink* is a noun.

Here are more examples:

I NEED SOME **HELP**.

In this sentence *help* is a noun.

I WILL **HELP** YOU.

In this sentence *help* is a verb.

HE IS A **TALL** MAN .

In this sentence *man* is a noun.

MAN! YOU REALLY DID IT THAT TIME !

In this sentence *man* is an interjection.

RUN!

In this sentence *run* is a verb.

HE WENT FOR A **RUN**.

In this sentence *run* is a noun.

The same sound or symbol can be used as different parts of speech and have different meanings.

A mistake some people make is to think, because they know one meaning or definition of the word being used, that they understand the word.

The person can then become quite puzzled when he does not understand the sentence in which the word is being used.

For example, a person is told, "The wind swept the boat down the river."

In this example the definition of the word swept which the person knows, is not the one being used.

Swept in this example means moved swiftly.

Many of the words in the language are homonyms so this sort of thing can happen often.

The answer is to look the word up in the dictionary.

You will find that it has a meaning that you had never come across before.

To make it simpler to learn English grammar, all you would have to do is to learn the parts of speech perfectly and understand that the language has many homonyms.

Once you have done this you would find that English grammar was very simple and that you had gained the ability to express yourself easily.

Drills

1. Look up the word *play* in the dictionary and count how many definitions it has.

2. How many different parts of speech can *play* be used as?

3. Think of three other words and find out how many definitions each of these have. How many parts of speech can they be used as?

CHAPTER FIVE

EXPRESSING YOURSELF WITH WORDS

Expressing Yourself with Words

You should now have a good understanding of words and the parts of speech.

The next step is putting it all together so that you can clearly express your thoughts and ideas and be able to understand written and spoken language.

Usually groups of several words are combined together to express thoughts and make it possible for communication to take place.

A very common way of expressing oneself is with an **expressed thought**.

HELLO.

OPEN MONDAY–FRIDAY

BEAUTIFUL

ME TOO

An **expressed thought** is a word or group of words that express a complete thought but which is not a sentence because it does not have a subject and verb.

Here are some more examples of expressed thoughts:

BREAKABLE

THIS SIDE UP

Some more examples are:

Milk and sugar?

Just milk, thanks.

Thanks a lot.

Well, I never!

Goodness me!

What a friendly person.

An expressed thought is not usually talked about in other grammar books, but it is a part of communication.

Sentences

Words are usually grouped together to form sentences.

A sentence has already been defined as a group of words put together to express a complete thought. A sentence is made up of at least a **subject** (some person, place or thing being talked about) and a **verb** (a word that shows action or state of being).

You have learned that there are parts of speech. There are also parts of a sentence.

If you know the parts of a sentence you will be able to understand and use sentences more easily.

Subject

The **subject** of a sentence is the person, place, thing, action or idea that is being talked about.

HE SEES THEM.
subject

STEVE OWNS A CAR.
subject

THE **TEA** IS HOT.
subject

Drills

1. Use a sheet of paper and write down ten sentences and underline the subject in each. Have your twin check your work.

2. Have your twin tell you some sentences. Spot the subject in each sentence and tell it to your twin. Do this until you can do it easily.

All sentences have a subject, even if it is not stated in the sentence. Like the sentence “Go!” The subject is understood to be *you*. “(You) go!”

The subject can be more than one person, place, thing, action or idea.

Paris and *Rome* are interesting cities to visit.

You or *I* must go.

Spring and *autumn* are my favorite seasons.

The way you can find the subject of a sentence if you are not sure is to find the verb and ask, *“Who or what (verb)?”*

The cat likes milk.

Who or what likes? The cat likes. That’s the subject.

Drills

1. Point out the subjects in the following sentences. (Take turns with your twin doing one sentence each.)

a. The boy waved at us.

b. New York is a big city.

c. Joe and Bill went to town to see the circus.

d. Cats love to hunt.

e. The weather has been warm.

f. Our car is parked over there.

g. The movie was very good.

h. He did not want to go.

i. I asked him to do me a favor.

j. That store has men's clothing.

2. Use a sheet of paper and write down five sentences. Show your twin the subject (or subjects) in each sentence.

Drill Answers

1. a. boy

   b. New York

   c. Joe, Bill

   d. Cats

   e. weather

   f. car

   g. movie

   h. He

   i. I

   j. store

Verb

A **verb** is a word or words that show action or state of being. The verb in a sentence states or asks something about what the subject is, does or has.

SHE **IS WALKING**.
verb

HE **LIES** IN THE SUN.
verb

IT IS ON THE TABLE.
verb

Drills

1. Use a sheet of paper and write down ten sentences. Underline the verb in each. Have your twin check your work.

2. Have your twin tell you some sentences. Spot the verb in each sentence and tell it to your twin. Do this until you can do it easily.

Remember that a sentence has at least a subject and a verb.

He *is* a smart guy.

They *went* west.

We *own* a lot of land.

Whose dog *is* that?

The sentences below have a subject and an intransitive verb.

John *runs*.

The man *awoke*.

Who *laughed*?

A sentence can have more than one verb.

The children *played* and *laughed* all day.

The men *walked* and *talked* together.

The girls in the show *danced* and *sang*.

In the pool they *swam* and *dove*.

The fire *hissed* and *popped*.

Drills

1. Point out the verbs in each of the following sentences. (Take turns with your twin doing one sentence each.)

a. She is carrying a large package.

b. They went to the game.

c. The boys were late.

d. Her typewriter is on the table.

e. They talked and laughed for a long time.

f. The movie starts at seven o'clock.

g. The dinner and movie were good.

h. Sam has two brothers.

i. Her father buys and sells used cars.

j. They found the cat in a tree.

2. Use a sheet of paper and write down five sentences. Show your twin the verb (or verbs) in each.

Drill Answers

1. a. is carrying

   b. went

   c. were

   d. is

   e. talked, laughed

   f. starts

   g. were

   h. has

   i. buys, sells

   j. found

Sometimes sentences also have an **object**.

There are two different kinds of objects. A **direct object** tells what the action of the verb results in, what it affects or what it is directed to.

SHE DREW **PICTURES**.
direct object

The action of drawing resulted in pictures.

SHE IS LIFTING THE **BOX**.

direct object

The action of lifting affects the box.

HE SEES **HER.**
direct object

The action of seeing is directed to her.

Here are some more examples of sentences with direct objects.

She is baking a *cake*.

(action of baking resulting in a cake)

He throws the *ball*.

(action of throwing affects the ball)

She liked *him*.

(action of liking directed at him)

A direct object answers the question "What?" or "Whom?" after a verb expressing action.

The carpenter fixed

This is not a complete sentence because it doesn't tell what the carpenter fixed. It is missing a direct object.

The carpenter fixed the *roof*.

What did the carpenter fix? He fixed the roof. *Roof* is the direct object.

We saw *her*.

Whom did we see? We saw her. *Her* is the direct object.

There can be more than one direct object in a sentence.

She loves *skiing* and *hiking*.

They need *books, pencils* and *paper*.

Drills

1. Use a sheet of paper and write down ten sentences with direct objects. Underline the direct object in each. Have your twin check your work.

2. Have your twin tell you some sentences with direct objects. Spot the direct object in each sentence and tell it to your twin. Do this until you can do it easily.

An **indirect object** is the person, place, thing, action or idea that the action of the verb is done to or done for.

SHE IS TELLING **HIM** HER NAME.
indirect object

The indirect object (him) is the person to which the action of the verb (is telling) is done.

SHE IS GIVING HER **DOG** A BONE.
indirect object

The indirect object (dog) is the thing for which the action of the verb (is giving) is done.

THE BOYS ASKED THE **MAN** A QUESTION.

indirect object

The indirect object (man) is the person to which the action of the verb (asked) is done.

A sentence can have an indirect object and a direct object.

John gave *her* a present.

This sentence has a subject (John), a verb (gave) and a direct object (present). It also has an indirect object, *her*.

The indirect object can be left out of the sentence and it would still make sense: John gave a present. But the direct object cannot be left out: John gave her.

An indirect object is a noun or pronoun that answers the question "to whom?" or "to what?" or "for whom?" or "for what?" the action of the sentence is done.

The clerk gave ***me*** my *change*.

The clerk gave what? Change. *Change* is the direct object.

To whom was the change given? Me. *Me* is the indirect object.

She baked ***Joe*** a cake.

She baked what? A cake. *Cake* is the direct object.

For whom was the cake baked? For Joe. *Joe* is the indirect object.

The indirect object can be more than one person, place or thing.

She told ***John*** and ***Henry*** the same thing.

Sentences don't have to have an object, but they often do.

Verbs like *be, seem, appear, become, taste, look, feel,* etc., are often followed by modifiers, not objects.

In the sentence "He looks happy," there is no object. The verb *looks* does not express action, it helps to express the state of being of the subject of the sentence—happy. *Happy* is a modifier, not an object.

In the sentence "The flowers are growing fast," there is no object. *Fast* is a modifier describing how the flowers are growing.

Drills

1. Use a sheet of paper and write down ten sentences with indirect objects. Underline the indirect object in each. Have your twin check your work.

2. Have your twin tell you some sentences with indirect objects. Spot the indirect object in each sentence and tell it to your twin. Do this until you can do it easily.

So you can see that sentences are formed in certain ways. They can be long or short, but they have to follow the basic parts of a sentence in order for communication to be clear.

For instance, if someone said, “Go I want to,” (instead of, “I want to go”) other people might have trouble understanding him. This is because he does not know or will not follow the right way to form sentences.

By knowing the parts of a sentence, you can clearly understand what others want to communicate with their sentences. You can also put together sentences which communicate exactly what you wish to say and which will be easily understood by others.

Drills

1. Tell your twin five sentences.

2. Tell your twin five sentences which contain verbs that are made of more than one word.

3. Make up a simple sentence and tell your twin what the subject is in the sentence.

4. Make up a simple sentence and tell your twin what the verb is in the sentence.

5. Make up a simple sentence which contains a direct object and tell your twin what the object is in that sentence.

6. Point out the subjects, verbs and objects in the following sentences. State whether the objects are direct or indirect objects. (Take turns with your twin doing one statement each.)

   a. The dog ate the food.

   b. She was tired.

   c. Rachel asked Bill a question.

   d. He threw the ball.

   e. I gave him the money.

   f. Grandfather built us a treehouse.

   g. The man saw the accident.

   h. The girl gave him a kiss on the cheek.

Drill Answers

6. a. dog—subject
   ate—verb
   food—direct object

   b. She—subject
   was—verb

   c. Rachel—subject
   asked—verb
   Bill—indirect object
   question—direct object

   d. He—subject
   threw—verb
   ball—direct object

   e. I—subject
   gave—verb
   him—indirect object
   money—direct object

   f. Grandfather—subject
   built—verb
   us—indirect object
   treehouse—direct object

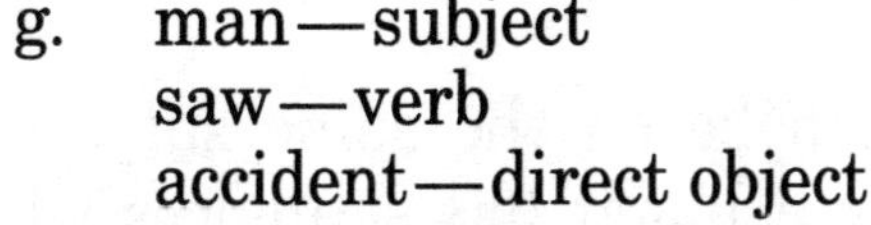

   g. man—subject
   saw—verb
   accident—direct object

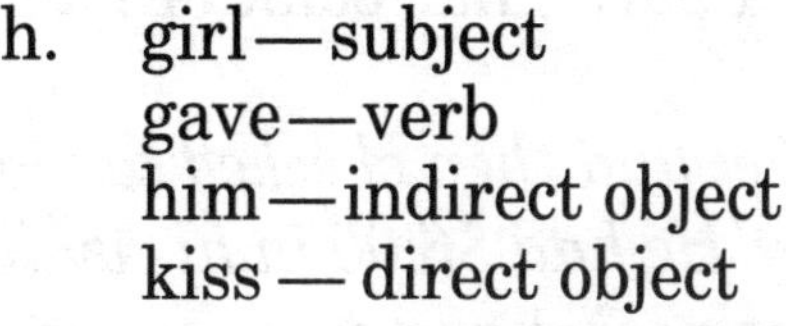

   h. girl—subject
   gave—verb
   him—indirect object
   kiss — direct object

Paragraphs

Paragraphs are usually made up of one or more sentences. These sentences are related to each other because they are about the same point (main idea).

A paragraph can be on the same subject as the one before or after it but it has sentences which are grouped together on a particular point or idea.

He put on his jacket and then checked to make sure he had enough money. He had $6.00 in his wallet so he put the wallet into his pocket and went outside.

That's a paragraph.

Now you're going off to discuss where he is going so it is a new idea and a new paragraph.

Once he got outside, he went down his street to the corner. His friend Joe met him there and they both headed for the movie theater.

Now you've discussed where he is going. Then, if you wanted to say that it was a long way to the theater, that could go in the paragraph on where he was going, but you would normally put it in a new paragraph.

A paragraph could actually be made up of one sentence if that sentence were all you were going to say on that point.

Once they got to the theater, they both bought their tickets and popcorn and went to find some front row seats so that they could watch the movie.

That's all you are going to say on that point so that would be the end of the paragraph.

Paragraphs are usually shown by indentation. Indentation means setting the letters of the first line in further from the rest of the lines in the paragraph.

This is indentation.

CHAPTER SIX:

PUNCTUATION

Punctuation

Punctuation is the system and the way of using marks (or symbols) in writing and printing that make the written communication clearer.

These marks are used to help you get the feeling of what is being written or printed.

If there were no punctuation marks ever used, it would be pretty difficult to understand what you are reading.

For example:

his mother said go to the store and he did at the store he bought bread butter and milk

This is how it would read with punctuation.

His mother said, "Go to the store," and he did. At the store he bought bread, butter and milk.

Punctuation marks help make written communication easier to understand.

This section will teach you many of the punctuation marks that we use.

Period 

(also called a *full stop*)

A **period** is used to show that a sentence is completed.

JOE IS SLEEPING.

PETE HAS A BROOM.

A period is used after numbers or letters to separate them from the words following.

BEFORE YOU LEAVE
1. CLOSE THE WINDOW

2. TURN OFF THE LIGHT
3. LOCK THE DOOR

A period shows that a word has been abbreviated (made shorter).

MONDAY

MON.

UNITED STATES OF AMERICA

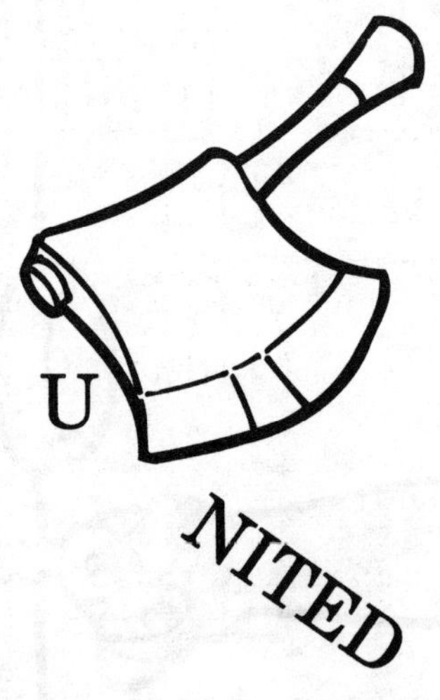

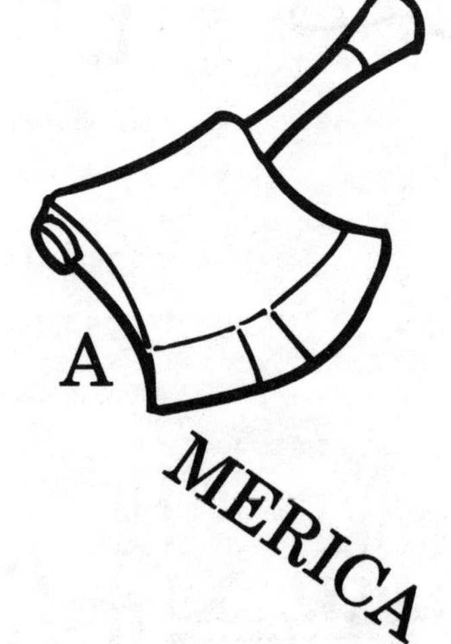

U.S.A.

CO. COMPANY

APT. APARTMENT

DEC. DECEMBER

When you read out loud a period tells you to make a full stop.

Drill

1. Use a sheet of paper and write down ten examples of how to use a period correctly. Show them to your twin.

Comma ,

A **comma** is used to separate words from each other.

THE BOYS ARE SWIMMING, DIVING
AND PLAYING BALL.

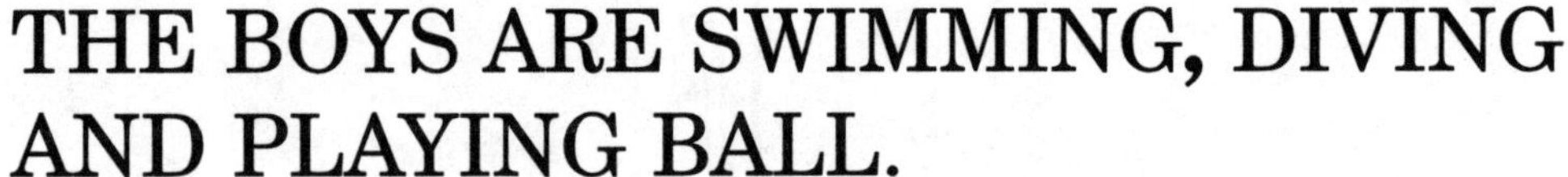

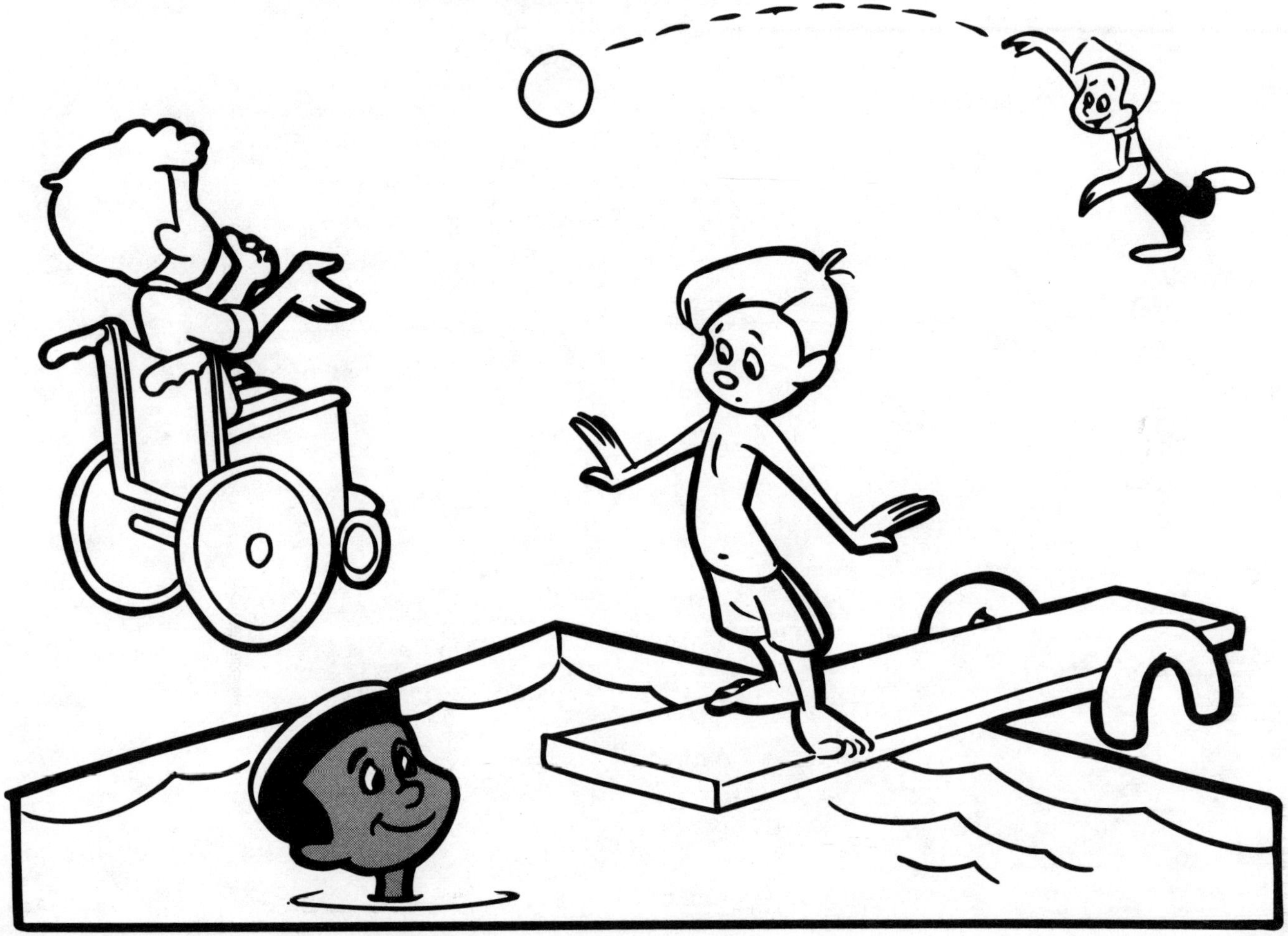

JOE HAS PENS, PAPER, PENCILS AND BOOKS.

TOM IS DIGGING, SALLY IS WATERING AND JOE IS PULLING WEEDS.

A comma is used to separate the parts of an address. The letter is addressed to Joe Jones, 302 Elm Street, Chicago, Illinois.

Joe Jones
302 Elm Street
Chicago, Illinois

A comma is used to separate the parts of a date.

TODAY IS THURSDAY, MARCH 15.

A comma is used after the greeting in a friendly letter.

Dear Mom,

Dear Joe,

A comma is used after the closing in a letter.

Love,
Your pal,
Yours truly,
Your friend,
Sincerely yours,

When you read out loud a comma tells you to take a small pause.

SHE LIKES TO DANCE, PLAY THE PIANO AND SING.

Drill

1. Use a sheet of paper and write down ten examples of the correct use of a comma. Show them to your twin.

Semicolon ;

A **semicolon** tells you to take a medium pause or stop. The stop you take with a semicolon is greater than the one you take with a comma and less than the one you take with a period.

IN THE WINTER HE GOES SKIING; IN THE SUMMER HE GOES SWIMMING.

THE CHILDREN OFTEN HELP AROUND THE HOUSE; NOT BECAUSE THEY HAVE TO, BUT BECAUSE THEY WANT TO.

A semicolon is used after the greeting in a slightly formal or respectful letter.

When you read out loud a semicolon tells you to take a medium pause or stop.

We stood in line for an hour; however, the game was well worth waiting for.

Drill

1. Use a sheet of paper and write down three examples of how to use a semicolon correctly. Show them to your twin.

Colon :

A **colon** is used before a list of items or details or before examples of things.

HER DUTIES INCLUDE THE FOLLOWING: TYPING LETTERS, ANSWERING THE PHONE AND TAKING MESSAGES.

A colon is used between hours and minutes when writing the time.

A colon is used after the greeting in a business letter.

When you read out loud a colon tells you to take a big pause or stop.

The basket contained: fruit, bread, ham, cheese, cookies, dishes and lemonade.

Drill

1. Use a sheet of paper and write down five examples of how to use a colon correctly. Show them to your twin.

Exclamation Point !

An **exclamation point** is used to show surprise or strong feeling.

SHE FELL DOWN.

SHE FELL DOWN!

WOW.
WOW!

Some more examples would be:

We won!

Oh my!

Ouch!

Wow! That is beautiful!

Do it right now!

Drills

1. Use a sheet of paper and write down five examples of the correct use of an exclamation point. Show them to your twin.

2. Write a short story or joke without using any punctuation marks. Have your twin read it aloud to you.

3. Use a sheet of paper and write down three different uses of a period. Show them to your twin.

4. Use a sheet of paper and write down six different uses of a comma. Show them to your twin.

5. Use a sheet of paper and write down three different uses of a semicolon. Show them to your twin.

6. Use a sheet of paper and write down three different uses of a colon. Show them to your twin.

7. Use a sheet of paper and write down two different uses of an exclamation point. Show them to your twin.

Question Mark ?

A **question mark** is used after a question.

IT LOOKS GOOD
DOESN'T IT?

WHAT IS
YOUR NAME?

WHERE IS MY DOG?

Drill

1. Use a sheet of paper and write down ten examples of the correct use of a question mark. Show them to your twin.

Quotation Marks 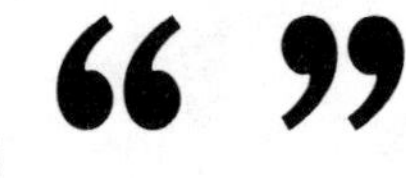

Quotation marks are used to show exactly what someone said.

SHE SAID,
"I LOVE ROSES."

Here are some more examples:

"I can't do this alone," said Bob.

"Get out of here!" she yelled.

He looked at me and said, "Let's go."

"Come here," I said.

He looked very big as he said, "No," so I ran away.

"Let her speak," said Bill, "she's important too."

A comma is used to separate what was said from the rest of the sentences in the examples above (unless that part of the sentence uses a different punctuation mark).

Quotation marks are used to show the titles of magazine articles, chapters of books, songs or poems.

SHE IS LISTENING TO
"HOME ON THE RANGE."

JOE IS READING A CHAPTER CALLED "TRAVELING IN EUROPE."

Here are some more examples:

He enjoyed reading a magazine article called "Plant Care."

"The Dancer" is my favorite poem.

"Christmas Eve" was the best chapter in the book.

Quotation marks can be used to show that a word is being referred to as a word.

SHE IS LOOKING UP “TO.”

Here are more examples:

I need to look up the word "biscuit."

She always misspells "their."

The word "that" is missing from the sentence.

There is a silent letter in the word "island."

Quotation marks are also used to show slang expressions, nicknames or humorous words.

THEY USED TO
CALL ME "SLUGGER."

Drills

1. Use a sheet of paper and write down three examples showing the correct use of a question mark. Show them to your twin.

2. Use a sheet of paper and write down three different ways that quotation marks can be used. Show them to your twin.

3. Correctly punctuate the following sentences. (Take turns with your twin doing one sentence each.)

a. Come here she said

b. He heard someone say I know the answer

c. I won she yelled

d. Did you hear him say Be quiet

e. I wonder said the boy will she ever get here

f. What a great day he exclaimed

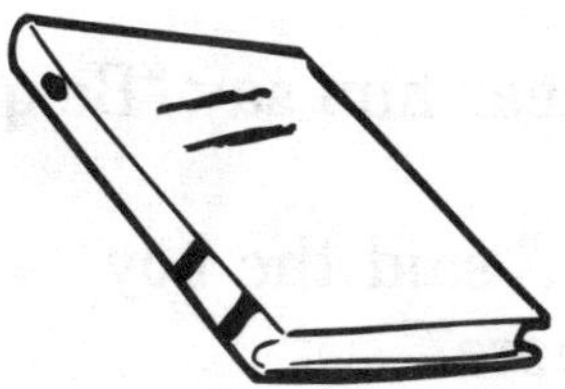

Drill Answers

3. a. "Come here," she said.

   b. He heard someone say, "I know the answer."

   c. "I won!" she yelled.

   d. Did you hear him say, "Be quiet"?

   e. "I wonder," said the boy, "will she ever get here?"

   f. "What a great day!" he exclaimed.

Single Quotation Marks ‘ ’

Single quotation marks are used inside double quotation marks when the sentence is already in double quotation marks.

HE SAID, "MY FAVORITE STORY IS 'THE SUN' BY D. H. LAWRENCE."

YOU'RE ALWAYS TELLING ME "YOU SHOULD LEARN TO COOK."

HE SAID "YOU'RE ALWAYS TELLING ME 'YOU SHOULD LEARN TO COOK.' "

Drill

1. Use a sheet of paper and write down five examples of how to use single quotation marks. Show them to your twin.

Apostrophe ’

An **apostrophe** is used to show that something is owned or belongs to somebody.

MARIA’S BIKE IS HERE.

THIS IS CRYSTAL’S BABY.

THE CHILDREN'S BALL WAS BIG.

An apostrophe can show that something is owned, in the following ways:

1. If the noun does not end in *s*, add *'s*.

Jim	Jim's
boy	boy's
children	children's
women	women's

2. If the noun is singular and ends in *s*, add *'* or *'s*.

Charles	Charles'	Charles's
boss	boss'	boss's

3. If the noun is plural and ends in *s*, add *'*.

girls	girls'
dogs	dogs'
ladies	ladies'

THE GIRLS' KITTEN WAS PLAYING.

An apostrophe is also used to show that a letter or letters have been left out of a word.

HE CANNOT LIFT IT.
HE CAN'T LIFT IT.

SHE IS NOT STANDING UP.
SHE ISN'T STANDING UP.

THE KITTEN WILL NOT COME DOWN.
THE KITTEN WON'T COME DOWN.

DO NOT CROSS THE STREET.
DON'T CROSS THE STREET.

Drill

1. Use a sheet of paper and write down ten examples of how to use an apostrophe correctly. Show them to your twin.

Parentheses ( )

Parentheses are used to insert or put additional data into a sentence.

THE FLOWERS (ROSES) SMELL GOOD.

THE FRUIT (4 PEARS AND 3 APPLES) IS ON THE TABLE.

Parentheses are used to show letters, numbers or symbols which are used to explain something.

SHE RECEIVED THREE (3) LETTERS.

TOM IS BORROWING FIVE DOLLARS ($5.00) FROM MIKE.

HE LIKES SPORTS (FOOTBALL, SOCCER AND BASKETBALL).

A single parenthesis can be used to separate things out of a sentence or to list things out.

ON THE TABLE THEY SAW:
1) BOOKS
2) BOTTLES
3) CUPS

SHE KNOWS HOW TO A) DANCE, B) PLAY THE PIANO AND C) SING.

Drill

1. Use a sheet of paper and write down ten examples of how to use parentheses correctly. Show them to your twin.

Drills

1. Use a sheet of paper and write down three examples of the correct use of single quotation marks. Show them to your twin.

2. Write out for your twin how you would show that something is owned, using the following words. (Take turns with your twin doing one word each.)

a. Mary
b. child
c. man
d. dog
e. Bill
f. children
g. men
h. girls
i. houses
j. countries

3. Use a sheet of paper and write down five other examples of the correct use of an apostrophe. Show them to your twin.

4. Use a sheet of paper and write down three examples of the correct use of parentheses. Show them to your twin.

5. Use a sheet of paper and write down three examples of the correct use of a single parenthesis. Show them to your twin.

Drill Answers

2. a. Mary's

   b. child's

   c. man's

   d. dog's

   e. Bill's

   f. children's

   g. men's

   h. girls'

   i. houses'

   j. countries'

Italics

Italics are a style of printing where the letters lean to the right.

ITALICS look like this.

Underlining is putting a line under a word or words.

This is underlining.

When you can't use italics you can use underlining instead.

Italics (or underlining) are used to emphasize a word or words.

SHE HAS ADDRESSED *HUNDREDS* OF LETTERS.
SHE HAS ADDRESSED HUNDREDS OF LETTERS.

JOE WILL *NOT* EAT.
JOE WILL <u>NOT</u> EAT.

Italics (or underlining) are used to show the titles of books, magazines and works of art.

SHE HAS A COPY OF *ALICE IN WONDERLAND*.
SHE HAS A COPY OF <u>ALICE IN WONDERLAND</u>.

THEY'RE GOING TO SEE *MODERN TIMES*.
THEY'RE GOING TO SEE <u>MODERN TIMES</u>.

Italics (or underlining) are used to show the names of planes, trains, ships and so on.

Italics (or underlining) are used to show that words are foreign words.

HE IS HAVING *CREPES* FOR LUNCH.
HE IS HAVING <u>CREPES</u> FOR LUNCH.

(*Crepes* are thin French pancakes.)

Italics (or underlining) can be used to show that a word is being referred to as a word.

Drill

1. Use a sheet of paper and write down ten examples using italics (or underlining) correctly. Show them to your twin.

Using Capital Letters

Capitalize the first word of a sentence or a direct quote.

The boy ran away.

John looked at me and said, "Come here."

Capitalize the pronoun "I."

Can you see why I did it?

A **proper noun** is the name of a particular person, place or thing. Proper nouns are capitalized.

Proper Nouns

John Smith

Susan Brown

John O'Casey

William McDonald

Mary Jones

San Diego

England

Snake River

Smith College

Detroit

Arizona

Pacific Ocean

Hollywood Boulevard

France

A **proper modifier** is a modifier formed from the name of a particular person, place or thing. Proper modifiers are also capitalized.

Proper Modifiers

Chinese vase

American people

Swiss cheese

Danish pastry

English tea

Smith's auto

Debbie's diner

Capitalize the names of ships, planes, trains, awards and heavenly bodies.

Queen Mary (ship)

The Dagger (plane)

The Silver Streak (train)

Jupiter (heavenly body)

Capitalize the first word and all the important words in titles of books, magazines, poems, short stories, movies, paintings, newspapers, articles and works of art.

The Wizard of Oz (book)
Saturday Evening Post (magazine)
"My Summer Vacation" (short story)
U.S.A. Today (newspaper)
"The Care and Feeding of Ducks" (article)
Mona Lisa (painting)

Capitalize the names of the days of the week, months and special holidays.

Monday
April
Halloween
Thanksgiving

Capitalize the names of nationalities, races and religions.

Japanese
American
Indian
Christian

Capitalize the names of organizations, groups, buildings, historical events or periods, documents and monuments.

Reed College
State Department
Garden Club
Empire State Building
Civil War
Dark Ages
Declaration of Independence

Capitalize titles of office or honor.

President Washington
Judge Parker
Reverend Moses
Doctor Miles

Abbreviations are capitalized when the words they stand for are capitalized.

U.S.A. (United States of America)
C.O.D. (Cash on Delivery)
U.K. (United Kingdom)
U.S.S. (United States Ship)

Capital letters are used for emphasis.

When I say, "Don't do it," I mean, "DO NOT DO IT!"

As you are working, make sure you LOOK at what you are doing.

Do not capitalize the names of school subjects except names of languages and course names followed by a number.

English
French
science
Science I
American History III

Do not capitalize north, south, east or west when they mean direction. Capitalize them when they mean sections of a country.

He came from the South. (section of a country)

He is headed south of town. (direction)

I live in the West. (section of a country)

I am traveling west. (direction)

Drills

1. Give your twin ten examples of words that would be capitalized.

2. Use capital letters correctly in each of the following examples.

a. new york state

b. i saw mount shasta.

c. portugal

d. the indian ocean

e. europe

f. she looked at the pacific ocean.

g. venus

h. *blue boy* (a painting)

i. he went west.

j. she came from the south.

k. african

l. spanish

m. the middle ages

n. a boy named tom

o. a small cat

p. the ocean

q. judge jones

r. aunt sue

s. asia

t. united kingdom

u. irish

v. the sky

w. nhl (national hockey league)

Drill Answers

2. a. New York State
   b. I saw Mount Shasta.
   c. Portugal
   d. the Indian Ocean
   e. Europe
   f. She looked at the Pacific Ocean.
   g. Venus
   h. *Blue Boy* (a painting)
   i. He went west.
   j. She came from the South.
   k. African
   l. Spanish
   m. the Middle Ages
   n. a boy named Tom
   o. a small cat
   p. the ocean
   q. Judge Jones
   r. Aunt Sue
   s. Asia
   t. United Kingdom
   u. Irish
   v. the sky
   w. NHL (National Hockey League)

Drill

1. Use a sheet of paper and write out the following paragraph with full punctuation.

tom was just walking away from his house when he saw his neighbor s dog tiger running down the street he yelled tiger but tiger didn t come tom started running after tiger tiger turned the corner and went down lemon street when tom got to lemon street he saw tiger digging in pine tree park tom said tiger what are you doing tiger barked and picked up a bone he had just dug up then he wagged his tail and walked happily home with tom

Drill Answers

Tom was just walking away from his house when he saw his neighbor's dog Tiger running down the street. He yelled, "Tiger!" but Tiger didn't come. Tom started running after Tiger. Tiger turned the corner and went down Lemon Street. When Tom got to Lemon Street he saw Tiger digging in Pine Tree Park. Tom said, "Tiger, what are you doing?" Tiger barked and picked up a bone he had just dug up, then he wagged his tail and walked happily home with Tom.

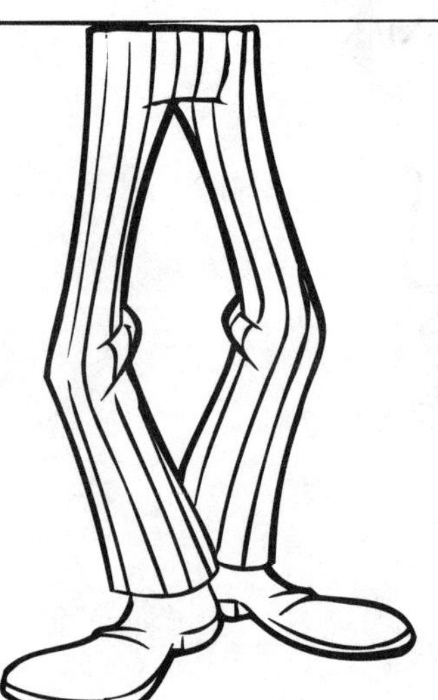

CHAPTER SEVEN:

WRITTEN AND SPOKEN COMMUNICATION

Written Communication

Much communication takes place in writing.

There are many different kinds of written material. There are books, encyclopedias, dictionaries, newspapers, magazines and many more.

One of the most common ways for people to communicate in writing is by letters.

A **letter** is a written or printed communication to another person or group of people.

It is very important that letters be clearly written. The intention of the person writing the letter must be clearly expressed so that it can be understood by the person receiving the letter.

A person who can communicate can easily express himself in letters so that the person receiving his letter understands what he has written and is eager to receive further communication from him.

If a letter is not written clearly, then the person receiving the letter won't understand it.

There are several parts to letters and all of them have names:

The **heading** consists of the sender's address and the date. It goes at the top right-hand corner of the letter.

5437 North Main
San Juan, Colorado 44792

24 April

The **inside address** is the name and address of the person to whom the letter is directed.

The **salutation** is the opening greeting to the person.

5437 North Main
San Juan, Colorado 44792

24 April

Julie Brown
2332 Main Street
Orange City, California 92689

Dear Julie,

The **complimentary close** is the "Yours truly" or "Sincerely," etc., used to show the end of the letter.

The **written signature** is the personally written signature of the person writing.

The **typed signature** is the name of the person writing the letter, typed out by a typist. If it was a business letter this would include the person's position in the business.

If the letter is typed by someone other than the person who wrote the letter then the initials of the person, followed by the initials of the typist, go at the bottom left of the letter.

Yours sincerely,

David Smith

David Smith
Manager

DS:ls

Here is an example of a business letter:

THE NEW CAR COMPANY
1310 Olympic Boulevard
Los Angeles, California 72631

March 1, 1992

Mr. Robert S. Johnson
Manager, Ace Car Sales
1350 Watchill Rd.
Texarkana, Arkansas 65532

Dear Mr. Johnson:

We were pleased to receive your order for ten of our newest model sports cars for your showroom.

We are happy to be able to tell you that these will be delivered to you next Tuesday afternoon.

I have enclosed a copy of our newest catalog for your information.

We look forward to doing further business with you in the future.

Yours sincerely,

Jeff Smith

Jeff Smith
Sales Manager

Friendly letters are written or typed in a similar way but they are not as formal. Here is an example of a friendly letter:

5437 North Main
San Juan, Colorado 44792

24 April

Julie Brown
2332 Main Street
Orange City, California 92689

Dear Julie,

I just thought I'd write and let you know how things were going since I haven't seen you for ages.

Last week I was at camp. I went with three of my friends from school. We were staying in cabins up in the mountains. We had a lot of fun going on hikes and having picnics for lunch. At night we would go outside and learn about the stars.

On the last night, we had a huge Western barbecue and dance! You would have liked it.

I took pictures while I was there so if you are able to come by next week I can show them to you.

Love, Sue

Letters, and all forms of written communication, should be laid out neatly in the center of the page, not all bunched up at one side or at the other end.

There is a way that letters should be written. Writing letters this way will put agreement between you and the person you are writing to.

Drills in Written Communication

The following drills will help you to understand how to write better.

1. With your twin look at the definition of *sentence*, on page 177, again.

2. Use a sheet of paper and write five examples that are not sentences. Show them to your twin. Now fix the examples so that they are sentences and show them to your twin.

3. Use a sheet of paper and write ten sentences that are correct and communicate clearly. Show them to your twin. Look back to the definition of *sentence* on page 177 if you are not sure that the sentences are correct.

4. Use a sheet of paper and write a paragraph about something you did today. Make sure your sentences are correct and that you use correct punctuation.

5. Take a short walk with your twin. Write several paragraphs about something you noticed on your walk. Show it to your twin.

6. Use a sheet of paper and write several paragraphs describing how to do something you know how to do well. Make sure it's very clear and communicates well. Show it to your twin.

7. Use a sheet of paper and write a short story, poem, a play, an article or essay using the information and skills you have learned by studying this book. Show it to your twin.

8. Write a letter to a friend correctly, using punctuation, sentences and paragraphs. Show it to your twin. Write several letters until you can easily write a letter correctly.

Spoken Communication

There are many forms of spoken communication. You hear spoken communication through conversations, the movies, radio, lectures, speeches and so on.

The first kind of spoken communication most people think of is conversation.

Conversation is the outflowing of communication and inflowing of communication. A conversation is always two-way.

WELL, WHAT DID YOU DO?

WE WENT UP TO THE LAKE AND WATER SKIED AND WENT FISHING AND CAMPING.

For a conversation to exist the person speaking must be able to express himself so the other person understands what he has said.

The person receiving the communication must be able to duplicate (make an exact copy of) and understand the words spoken to him.

For spoken communication to be successful, you have to understand what is said.

A person who knows he can express himself and be understood is able to speak to a person or group easily and enjoyably.

It's all part of **communication**!

Drills

1. Have a conversation with your twin paying attention to the way the communication is put together.

2. Go and talk to someone who has not studied this book, paying attention to the way the communication is constructed.

3. Do this drill again until you are sure of the purpose and importance of correct construction of communication.

Summary

One *can* communicate with another person and be understood and can receive another's communication and understand.

Communication in speech and writing is made possible only by agreements concerning the use of words and language and this is why we study grammar.

Grammar makes communication possible.

The only way to understand is through communication.

Being in communication has a lot to do with being alive. If you really understand and use the established system of spoken and written communication you will be able to take part in life and really enjoy it. You will be able to get things done because you can communicate.

And that's a goal worth aiming for.

CONGRATULATIONS!

Congratulations on having completed the *Grammar and Communication for Children* book.

Being able to express yourself so that what you write and say is easily understood by others and being able to really understand what you read and hear is something that will help you for the rest of your life. What you have learned is very valuable and you should *use* this data every day and in everything you do.

Apply these new skills in your life and be successful in your communications with others. That is what grammar is for!

Important Information for Parents and Teachers

Grammar as taught in schools can be rough for children to learn.

Earlier grammar texts have defined grammar as a *"study" of rules* instead of defining it in terms of *use*. This gives an entirely wrong frame of reference for grammar and can make it seem pointless as a subject. What child would want to learn a bunch of rules? Without learning the *value* and *purpose* of grammar, it can appear to be just another thing that the teachers or schools are forcing the child to learn (when he would rather be doing something *he* wants to do).

A number of grammar books currently in use in schools were looked at and this is what was found: one defined grammar as "primarily the study of the forms of words and their relationship to each other" and three other grammar texts entirely omitted a definition for the word. It's very hard to learn a subject when the name of the subject itself is either not defined or is incorrectly defined!

So the word *grammar* had to be defined as something one *uses* in everyday speech and reading and writing, not something which was the monopoly of the grammarians. The whole point about grammar is that it exists to facilitate and enhance meaningful communication between and amongst people. It really has no other useful purpose.

This book starts off giving the reader the *use* and *value* of grammar.

It contains a simplification of the basic concepts of grammar as developed by L. Ron Hubbard. A lot of the complexity of grammar, as traditionally presented, has been stripped away to make it possible to learn and *use* the subject to better one's life.

Grammar is a basic building block to being able to study or learn or accomplish anything. Without a good ability to communicate and make oneself understood, one will not get far in life.

Thus this book has been published to give children a way to learn grammar that is easy and fun.

The information is given to the reader one step at a time, without giving him a lot of things to learn all at once that are over his head.

Getting the Most Out of the Book

In working with a child to help him learn grammar it will help if you first read the book yourself and get familiar with its contents.

In giving this book to your child and in working with him to get through the book, there is one very important datum about study which a parent or teacher must know:

THE ONLY REASON A PERSON GIVES UP A STUDY OR BECOMES CONFUSED OR UNABLE TO LEARN IS BECAUSE HE HAS GONE PAST A WORD THAT WAS NOT UNDERSTOOD.

The confusion or inability to grasp or learn comes AFTER a word that the person did not have defined and understood.

Here's an example. "It was found that when the crepuscule arrived the children were quieter and when it was not present they were much more noisy." You see what happens. You think you don't understand the whole idea, but the confusion comes only from one word you didn't know, *crepuscule*, which means the time from sunset to dark.

The datum about not going by a word that one does not understand is the most important datum in the whole subject of study. Every subject a person has taken up and then abandoned or done poorly with had its words which the person failed to get defined. It is the most important barrier to study and a parent or teacher should be familiar with this data.

Handling Trouble

If the child starts to have trouble getting the data, gets confused, feels like throwing the book down or giving up on it, it is because of a word he went by that he did not know the meaning of. If this should occur then help the child by getting him to go back to where he was last doing well with the material and right at that point, or just before that will be a word he didn't get. It needs to be found and then looked up and properly defined. There could be more than one.

"Twins"

The book is best studied with another person (called a "twin"). A twin is a study partner. Two twins would go through this whole book together, reading the text and doing all the drills together. Doing the drills is very, very important—remember it is the ability to *apply* the data that is important in study, not just learning a lot of data that you cannot then do anything with.

If it is not possible for the child or student to study the book with a twin, then he can study the book himself and write down all the answers to the drills. Sometimes the drills call for another person and so minimally he would need a parent or teacher or friend to help him with these drills.

Use in School Curricula

Numerous schools across the United States and throughout the world now use Mr. Hubbard's educational materials to promote faster learning with increased comprehension.

Further Information

If you or your child or student encounter any difficulties in reading this book there are addresses of schools and institutions listed at the back of this book which will provide any assistance needed. They will be happy to answer any questions or give you further information about these new advances in learning.

The whole idea of this grammar text is to enable a person to *use* the data in his speech and writing to help clearly express himself and allow him to understand the communication of others, whether it is verbal or written. That is the only real purpose for the subject.

Let's look forward to a society that *can* communicate!

About the Author

L. Ron Hubbard was no stranger to education. Although his main profession was that of a writer, in a long, event-filled and productive life, he spent thousands of hours researching, lecturing and teaching in the field of education.

He was born in Tilden, Nebraska on March 13, 1911, and his early years were spent in the frontier of Montana. As the son of a US Naval officer, he was well on the way to becoming a seasoned traveler by the age of eight, and by the time he was nineteen he had logged over a quarter of a million miles.

He enrolled in George Washington University in 1930, to study mathematics and engineering. But his was not a quiet academic life. He took up flying in the pioneering days of aviation, and was soon renowned for his barnstorming feats. He simultaneously worked as a free-lance reporter and photographer. He further directed expeditions to the Caribbean, a pivotal mineralogical survey on the island of Puerto Rico, and charted inland waterways through British Columbia. In short, the world was his classroom and he studied voraciously, gathering the experience that provided the background for his later writings and discoveries.

Drawing upon these adventures, he produced a variety of stories and novels to establish himself as one of the foremost names in popular literature.

The proceeds from this work, in turn, funded his main line of research—how to improve the human condition. His nonfiction works cover such diverse subjects as drug rehabilitation, marriage and family, success at work, statistical analysis, public relations, art, marketing and much, much more.

But he did more than write books—he also delivered over 2,400 lectures and conducted courses to impart his own discoveries to others. However, in order to learn, one must be able to read and understand. Therefore, L. Ron Hubbard tackled the problem of teaching others how to study. That research uncovered the basic reason for the failure of a student to grasp any subject. Mr. Hubbard further discovered the primary barriers to full comprehension, and developed methods by which anyone can improve the ability to learn and to *apply* data. He wrote a considerable body of work on this subject, which he termed Study Technology.

L. Ron Hubbard's advanced technology of study is now used by more than 74,000 teachers, to bring a new era of learning to over 3.7 million students in universities and school systems internationally. To meet the worldwide demand for the first truly workable technology of how to study, his educational materials have been translated into twelve languages. Organizations delivering L. Ron Hubbard's Study Technology have been established in over 60 different countries around the world on 6 continents.

Although L. Ron Hubbard departed this life on January 24, 1986, his work most certainly lives on, and his contributions to the field of education have meant new hope, better understanding and increased ability for millions of students and educators everywhere.

Additional Books by L. Ron Hubbard

Learning How to Learn · For children, knowing how to read and being able to understand and apply what they read is the real key to success in their lives. With the simple steps taught in this book, written for young students, learning can become an exciting and rewarding experience.

How to Use a Dictionary · This book provides students with the means to get the most out of their education through the use of the dictionary. Students learn everything from finding words quickly to understanding the symbols in dictionaries. It opens doors for those who would otherwise be unable to understand even the simplest of terms.

Study Skills for Life · Written for preteens and young teenagers, this book teaches students how to use what they are studying so they can attain the goals they set for themselves. Using these skills, they can break the barriers to learning.

Basic Study Manual · Whether you're going to college or starting a career, you need the ability to apply anything that you study, so you can do what you want in life. Using these skills, you can improve your concentration, improve your ability to learn and enjoy what you are studying.

All of these books are available as correspondence courses.

When a person can learn and think for himself/herself the world is an open book.

Index

APPLIED SCHOLASTICS INTERNATIONAL

INTERNATIONAL TRAINING CENTER — CORPORATE HEADQUARTERS

11755 RIVERVIEW DRIVE • ST. LOUIS, MISSOURI 63138 USA • VOICE: 314 355 6355 FAX: 314 355 2621

CONTINENTAL AND NATIONAL OFFICES

EDUCATION ALIVE AFRICA
PO BOX 30791
KYALAMI 1684
SOUTH AFRICA
+2711 702 2208

APPLIED SCHOLASTICS AUSTRALIA, NEW ZEALAND & OCEANIA
89 JONES STREET,
SUITE 64
ULTIMO,
NEW SOUTH WALES 2007
AUSTRALIA
+612 928 01023

APPLIED SCHOLASTICS BENELUX
FARENHEITSTRAAT 99
AMSTERDAM 1097
NETHERLANDS
+31 20 67 90668

APPLIED SCHOLASTICS CANADA
12 WESTVIEW
TORONTO, ONTARIO
M4B 3H8
CANADA
416 463 9950

APPLIED SCHOLASTICS CIS
B. GALUSHKINA STR. 19A
MOSCOW 129301
RUSSIA
+7 095 507 84 09

APPLIED SCHOLASTICS CZECH REPUBLIC
OPLETALOVA 36
PRAGUE 1, 110 00
CZECH REPUBLIC
+42 02 24 21 8684

APPLIED SCHOLASTICS DENMARK
NØRREGADE 26
1165 COPENHAGEN K
DENMARK
+45 33 32 36 80

APPLIED SCHOLASTICS EASTERN UNITED STATES USA
727 432 3233

APPLIED SCHOLASTICS EUROPE
NØRREGADE 26
1165 COPENHAGEN K
DENMARK
+45 33 32 3680

APPLIED SCHOLASTICS GERMANY
GROSSER WEG 3
30826 GARBSEN
GERMANY
+49 5131 4465 36

APPLIED SCHOLASTICS GREECE
MEGALOU ALEXANDROU 72
NEA SMYRNI
ATHENS 17122
GREECE
+301 93 25 400

APPLIED SCHOLASTICS HUNGARY
PF 321
BUDAPEST 1437
HUNGARY
+3630 900 3488

APPLIED SCHOLASTICS ITALY & MEDITERRANEO
VIA LEONCAVALLO 8
MILANO 20131
ITALY
+39 022 85 10 139

APPLIED SCHOLASTICS JAPAN
2 32 18 101, YOGA
SETAGAYA-KU
TOKYO, 158 0097
JAPAN
+81 3 3707 9297

APPLIED SCHOLASTICS LATIN AMERICA
RIO ELBA 10 INT. 101-A
CUAUHTEMOC,
CUAUHTEMOC
MEXICO D.F. 06500
MEXICO
+5255 5211 8452

APPLIED SCHOLASTICS LATVIA
ABAVAS STR. 21
RIGA LV-1004
LATVIA
+371 34 761 9149

APPLIED SCHOLASTICS MALAYSIA
15 LORONG BUKIT RAJA
TAMAN SEPUTEH
KUALA LUMPUR, 58000
MALAYSIA
+603 2274 5747

APPLIED SCHOLASTICS NEW ZEALAND
13 SUTTON CRESCENT
PO BOX 63052
PAPATOETOE, AUCKLAND
NEW ZEALAND
+649 278 4077

APPLIED SCHOLASTICS SWEDEN
KALLFORSVÄGEN, 40
BANDHAGEN 12432
SWEDEN
+486 649 4191

APPLIED SCHOLASTICS TAIWAN
2ND FLOOR
147 SAN MIN RD.
TAIPEI, 105
TAIWAN, R.O.C.
+886 2 276 99254
APPLIED SCHOLASTICS
UK ENGLAND
+44 1342 301 902

APPLIED SCHOLASTICS WESTERN UNITED STATES USA
714 348 9162

WWW.APPLIEDSCHOLASTICS.ORG • E-MAIL: EDUCATION@APPLIEDSCHOLASTICS.ORG